D1621160

GOD'S FIFTH COLUMNIST
&
OTHER WRITINGS

FREDERICK NEUMANN

GOD'S
FIFTH COLUMNIST
&
OTHER WRITINGS

FREDERICK NEUMANN

With Introductory Essays by
P. L. Berger & F. L. Battles

MARCHAM MANOR PRESS
APPLEFORD ABINGDON BERKS

Set in 10 point Times 1 point leaded
and printed in Great Britain by
University Tutorial Press, Foxton, Near Cambridge

Contents

Foreword

THE SELECTION in this book tries to present a characteristic sample of the work of my late husband Frederick Neumann, over a period of twenty years from 1944 to 1964. Two dates should be specially mentioned. The title-paper 'God's Fifth Columnist' was written in the McCarthy time in 1952 and the sermon 'Thanksgiving on a Day of Mourning' was delivered on November 24, 1963, two days after the death of President Kennedy. With the exception of the essay 'Fundamental Differences Between Judaism and Christianity' and 'God's Fifth Columnist' all papers were composed originally for the spoken word, most of them as lectures to groups of people of very diverse educational, social and religious—even atheistic— backgrounds. The talks were usually followed by lively discussion. Most of the sermons at the end of the volume were preached at Bushwick Avenue Congregational Church.

Up to 1952 the Bible quotations were taken from the King James Version and from then on from the American Revised Standard Version. Occasionally other translations, sometimes the author's own, were substituted. As to the text itself, we have left certain stylistic inconsistencies and incidental references to contemporary events as they are found in the manuscripts left by Frederick Neumann at his death.

I want to thank the many friends who helped me at every step of this editorial venture, especially Dr. Ford L. Battles of Pittsburg, Dr. Peter L. Berger of New York, Dr. Leo Kohorn of Bolton, England, and Dr. Daniel D. Williams of New York. I wish also to thank the editor of the *Hartford Quarterly* for permission to reproduce Professor Berger's article which has been slightly revised for book form. Though they are not mentioned by name, I have not forgotten the help I received from those friends who assisted me in retyping and copying the difficult manuscripts.

Mr. Gervase Duffield, whose advice and painstaking work in the publication and production of this book, has also earned our gratitude.

Brooklyn, New York, December 1971.   Edith Neumann.

1. Frederick Neumann, 1899-1967

Peter L. Berger

FREDERICK NEUMANN was born in Vienna on January 10, 1899. He grew up in that city during the period of its last cultural flourishing, a period of intense intellectual ferment and profound moral crisis. This background left its lifelong imprint on the man and on his thought. Neumann studied philosophy at the universities of Vienna and Freiburg/Breisgau at the time when these witnessed the genesis of the three philosophical movements that have turned out to be decisive ever since—phenomenology, existentialism and neo-positivism. Among Neumann's immediate teachers were Husserl, Heidegger and Gomperz. He obtained his doctorate at Vienna, with a dissertation on Lotze.

Neumann's family background was Jewish. He became a Christian as an adult, under the influence of Kierkegaard, to whom he acknowledged a deep indebtedness even in his later years. It was in the wake of his conversion that Neumann renounced the possibility of an academic career and put himself in the service of the Christian faith, a decision that crucially changed the course of his life and from which he never deviated. He lived in Vienna as a free-lance lecturer and as an evangelist for the Swedish Israel Mission. In the mid-1930's he spent some time in Yugoslavia as a missionary, then returned to Vienna, this time in the service of the British Jews Society. In 1927 he was married to Edith Spitzer, who became not only his companion in his chosen life, but his most important collaborator through many difficult years.

After the German occupation of Austria in 1938 the British Jews Society enabled the Neumanns' emigration to England, where Neumann was ordained as a Congregational minister. From 1939 to 1947 he served as a missionary in Haifa, Palestine. He came to America in 1948, as associate director of the Newcomers Christian Fellowship, an organisation that devoted itself to the care of newly arrived refugees in New York. Neumann was then called to the pulpit of the Bushwick Avenue Congregational Church, in Brooklyn.

1

His visiting professorship at Hartford coincided with the last years
of his ministry.   It is pertinent to observe that Neumann's appoint-
ment at Hartford was the only academic position ever held by him.
His work at Hartford was a source of much joy to him.   During his
final illness his thoughts repeatedly returned to Hartford, particularly to his students, for whom he felt a concern that was as much
pastoral as academic.

Neumann's early philosophical work was strongly marked by the
double influence of phenomenology and existentialism.   He was
interested in a reinterpretation of the early dialogues of Plato and
had begun a work on this subject.   Two philosophical problems
occupied his attention for many years—the problem of humour and
the problem of time.   Both problems became intertwined with his
theological interests and reappeared in many forms in his work—
lectures, exegeses and sermons.   Indeed, during most of Neumann's
life it is well nigh impossible to separate his philosophical from his
theological thought.   He loved Tertullian's notion of the *anima
naturaliter christiana*, and in his own thinking there was a natural
fusion of theologising and philosophising.

It is very difficult to locate Neumann's theological thought in
terms of contemporary alignments.   His thought was original and
solitary.   He was as uninterested in being orthodox as in being
fashionable, thus inevitably misunderstood in a situation in which
these interests (sometimes separately, sometimes in conjunction)
dominate the theological scene.   Neumann greatly respected Barth
and Tillich, but felt himself decisively separated from both on essential questions.   He was radically liberal in his utilisation of
Biblical scholarship, but his theological positions could not be
described either in terms of liberalism or of neo-orthodoxy.   He
was very much at home with patristic Christianity, with a particular
affinity to Tertullian, and equally so with the thought of the
Reformation.   He felt very close to the thought of Thomas à
Kempis, and had a lifelong interest in both Christian and non-
Christian mysticism.

With some hesitation, it is possible to indicate two very broad
trends in Neumann's theological thought.   The first is from a highly
individualistic understanding of Christianity, as first mediated to
him through Kierkegaard, to an increasingly churchly understanding.   This trend, of course, is reflected in his external career, from
unattached Christian intellectual to missionary and minister in a

historical denomination (to which, incidentally, Neumann had a strong, albeit penultimate, commitment). The early understanding is still strongly evident in one of his few published works, *Die Judenfrage und der christliche Jude* (1935). The later trend is evident, among other things, in his decreasing interest in the question of the 'Christian Jew'—the place of the Christian, whatever his origin, was, for Neumann, in the Christian Church—and the important questions of the Christian life became, for him, the questions that concerned the Church as such. Neumann's move from the thoroughly sterile (and, to boot, anti-Semitic) milieu of Austrian Lutheranism to that of Anglo-Saxon Protestantism is not irrelevant in this connection.

The second trend is more difficult to delineate, though probably more important. That is a trend from an existentialistic or dialectical theology to an ever deeper concern with ontology. If there is any theme that holds together Neumann's last theological thinking, it is the quest for the formulation of a Christian ontology. This trend is readily evident in the few lectures published in the *Hartford Quarterly* ('Ecclesiastes—Philosopher Without Propositions,' I, 3, 1961, 35-49; 'A Sermon for Trinity,' III, 1, 1962, 37-41; 'The Devil's Prayer—A Lyrical Play in One Act,' V, 4, 1965, 5-26), particularly in the paper on 'Faith and Conscience' and in the exegetical essay on Ecclesiastes, the latter culminating in the startling conclusion that the central question of Ecclesiastes is the age-old question of Greek philosophical inquiry—*ti to on?* The same theme was pursued by Neumann in his Hartford lectures on Genesis. It was also at the centre of his intense interest in the work of Eric Voegelin, and in the relationship between the Old Testament and the mythological thought of the ancient Near East. It had been Neumann's intention to develop this theme after his retirement in a work on the Trinity. The time for this was not given to him.

Neumann chose a life that did not entail outward 'success'. This personal decision has had the consequence that very little of his thought has seen the light of day in print. He has left no book. There are some scattered essays and articles available in printed form, and some are here added from the posthumous papers. Neumann's thought was transmitted in the most private way—in conversations—and publicly in lectures, sermons and, in the last few years, his teaching at Hartford. It is pertinent to point out here what vast resources of scholarship were invested by Neumann in his regular,

B

weekly sermon preparation—always without any regard for the numbers or the status of those who made up the audience of these sermons. The thought of Frederick Neumann, in an altogether un-modern way, was transmitted through oral, face-to-face communication.

The style of this communication, of course, varied with the occasion. Thus Neumann never used the pulpit to parade his erudition, and only a most careful study of his sermons would reveal the scholarly work that had gone into their preparation. But in his conversations and his academic lectures there were a few highly characteristic features, which were also features of his thought. These were catholicity, sharpness and wit. Quite apart from Neumann's personal tolerance for views that diverged from his own, his thought was open, as much to the richness of the various Christian traditions as to the varieties of secular philosophy. At the same time, Neumann's thought was sharp. He was devoted to consistency and to lucidity (in this, perhaps, a Calvinist in a very fundamental way!). And, ever again, there were eruptions of wit, as trenchant as compassion permitted. Neumann was a great admirer of Karl Kraus, the Viennese satirist, and occasionally he permitted himself the pleasures of both satire and irony. But Neumann's wit always ended with humour, with the specifically Christian form of laughter, which is the underside of joy.

In Frederick Neumann* we have lost a wise man and a Doctor of the Church. In the ambience of the Church, in a Christian understanding of wisdom, we may be consoled by the knowledge that nothing is ever lost that is done or thought before God. It is in the same context that we may recall, in memory of Frederick Neumann, the consolation of Ecclesiastes:

> I have also seen this example of wisdom under the sun, and it seemed great to me. There was a little city with few men in it; and a great king came against it and besieged it, building great siegeworks against it. But there was found in it a poor wise man, and he by his wisdom delivered the city. Yet no one remembered that poor man. But I say that wisdom is better than might, though the poor man's wisdom is despised, and his words are not heeded. The words of the wise man heard in quiet are better than the shouting of a ruler among fools (9: 13-17, RSV).

*He died May 13, 1967, in Brooklyn, New York.

2. Frederick Neumann and His Work

Ford Lewis Battles

IT IS GIVEN ONLY to a few great Christians to have a personal ministry beyond the bounds of death. Frederick Neumann was by human standards an obscure man known only to a very few privileged persons in Europe and America. As a man's life goes, his was a failure: he was rewarded neither with economic success, nor with academic honour, nor even with ecclesiastical station. The end of his life was spent in ministering to a tiny flock in a mouldering section of Brooklyn, with several years of part-time lecturing in Old Testament at the Hartford Seminary Foundation. Surely this man deserved far better at the hands of men than he ever received!

But this sternly humble man would sharply censure us for saying this. We would be guilty of completely misunderstanding his 'following of Christ' if we were to scold the world for overlooking him. There is another sense (and he would be the last to claim this) in which Frederick Neumann could be called a success beyond all customary understanding of that term. Fortunately for us, his witness to Jesus Christ has not gone unrecorded. He has left a rich and lively expression of his faith in the essays and sermons from which the present collection has been chosen. To his widow, Dr. Edith Neumann, has fallen the task of preparing these texts for publication. Those who read the pages of this book can thus come to know, almost as intimately as those who knew him in the flesh, a truly great Christian. More important than this, though, a reader might find there his 'tutor unto Christ', even as Frederick Neumann found his own in the pages of Søren Kierkegaard.

For many who read this book no introduction will be necessary, if they are willing patiently to read and reread, ponder and reponder, the author's simple but deep thoughts. But it may be helpful to point to a few matters especially in the longer essays, which might otherwise be overlooked or only partly grasped.

Pilgrimage

LET us direct our attention first to several pieces which most explicitly speak of Frederick Neumann's personal pilgrimage, and

5

of the way in which his inheritance was transformed. 'Looking Back,' 'On Luther's Spiritual Development Before the Reformation,' and 'Fundamental Differences between Judaism and Christianity' may be placed in this group.

Setting aside momentarily his wonted reticence toward talking about himself, Dr. Neumann sketches simply and quietly the pilgrimage of a young Jew of Vienna to Jesus Christ. His early agnosticism, the product of an excellent humanist education, led him in his late teens to search some of the classic philosophers for a real and substantial fundament, but it was only upon picking up the writings of Søren Kierkegaard that the final struggle to faith was initiated. Gradually all of the insistent demands on external criteria for religious certainty dissolved when he came to realise that faith in Christ is a matter of conscience, of responsible choice.

Conversion was only the beginning, however, of a life-long growth in faith. Daily Frederick Neumann died to himself that he might rise with Christ, who in his suffering made the supreme sacrifice for men, thus embodying God's love. Frederick Neumann sees in his own home-coming a paradigm of the profound homesickness of young people in whom God has implanted a deep-seated dissatisfaction with a world, Godless, spiritless and stale. Or rather, our author sees in Jesus Christ's facing and triumph over evil (the 'world') the paradigm of the homecoming that God holds out to the whole creation.

In these brief lines we are introduced to the personal ground on which rests all that Dr. Neumann has written. When he comes to trace Martin Luther's spiritual development, he feels a kindred spirit, despite the great contrasts of time and place. Yet all the treasures of our spiritual inheritance—whether of Luther or Kierkegaard or the great host of past Christians—must be approached by us if we are to make any headway in the spiritual life.

Coming as he did to the Christian faith directly from Judaism, Dr. Neumann pondered repeatedly the great mystery of Jew and Christian. In essays such as the one here published, in commentaries, and in his sermons, he strove to express his conviction that in Christ Jesus the whole revelation of God is summed up. This he did gently, firmly, never polemically, always aware of the symbiosis between the two great religious communities. The secret of his biblical exegesis lies in part in his grasp of the continuity of these two covenants both in history and individual experience.

Faith

FREDERICK NEUMANN was first of all a pastor: his theology flowed from that office. His sermons expounded the grand themes of the faith in the simplest language for his congregation. Thus, his sermons are the best place to read his theology. But occasionally he chose to express his theology explicitly in longer and more sustained forms. Our second group of essays is comprised of such pieces. Perhaps 'Why Is God?' should be read first, as a brief meditation on the mystery of the Trinity. Then the reader may wish to turn to the twin-essay, 'The Dialogue between God and Man', which plumbs the depths of freedom. Read these pieces slowly, out loud; do not be discouraged at first sight, for their meaning will come.

In 'Why Is God?' drawing upon Kierkegaard, Forsyth, Barth, Tillich, and upon such classic theologians as Irenaeus and Augustine, Frederick Neumann meditates in a deeply original way on the mystery of the Trinity. Taking the simple statement of 1 John, 'God is love' as his theme, he sets the Cross within the eternal familial life of the Three Persons. How is God love? Simply:

  i. The Father loves;

  ii. The Son returns love;

  iii. The Holy Spirit is love.

Upon this ineffable love—beyond any human explaining, but within the grasp of our minds through Jesus Christ the starting point of theology—must rest the fellowship of eternal love to which we are called:

  i. God demands of us trust, obedience, love;

  ii. In self denial we return through time to him,

  iii. And come to participate in the divine life of glorious, everlasting love.

The crossing of the Red Sea by the Israelites with its earliest interpretation in the Song of Miriam and the subsequent interpretation by the Deuteronomist serves as the Scriptural foundation for Dr. Neumann's twin essay on God and man, 'The Dialogue between

God and Man'. Miriam's Song praised God for his deliverance of
the fleeing Israelites. In this event and in all events of human
history and of individual life, God speaks to man. His words
always come through concrete situations and call us to respond to
him in and through those situations. Thus the whole of life, the
whole of human existence is a dialogue with God. How would
God have us respond to him? The struggle to make proper
response to him is dramatically sketched in the Ten Commandments which reveal our shifts to avoid an answer of humble submission to him. Dr. Neumann does not begin with a hypothetical,
flattering notion of human freedom: he resolutely faces the gulf
between God and fallen man, who must somehow be utterly shorn
of his supposed self-sufficiency to come into true freedom. As
Paul teaches, the law sets us free to obey God, but then, mysteri-
ously, sin proves stronger than freedom. It is in response to God's
Word in Jesus that we come to know true freedom, a future freedom promised to us, not a present freedom. It is a freedom Spirit-
given in our death-and-life communion with Christ, crucified and
risen.

God is Spirit; God is love. Yes, but these two simple statements are meaningless apart from history, apart from the experience of Israel which culminates in Jesus of Nazareth and is brought
to us in the Church.

In these two brief essays our author has ranged through the
whole of human history and experience. He has reviewed all the
false answers which men in their cleverness have set forth. He has
set the freedom of God and of man in that dialogue where alone it
can exist and be understood.

Conscience

THE long dialogue from which this collection of essays takes its
title, 'God's Fifth Columnist', lays open the heart of Frederick
Neumann's faith. In what is really an interior dialogue, at once in
the literary tradition of Plato, of the medieval conversations between body and soul, and of John Bunyan's *Pilgrim's Progress*, our
author threads his way through the modern jungle of false deities
and tempting idolatries, stripping from our existence as he proceeds the superficial trappings we so often mistake for truth.
Written in 1952, the piece commences with political conversation

characteristic of the immediate post-World War II era; the metaphor 'Fifth Columnist', born of the Spanish Civil War, was the common term during and after World War II for subversive agents at work for the enemy in the heart of the homeland.

The dialogue should be read aloud, and in several more than the four sittings he has cast it in, to be fully grasped. Then the reader can experience something of Frederick Neumann as he was in life. To the few who were privileged to know him and talk with him there are many echoes of real remembered conversations on these pages. His gentle but telling humour, his impatience with arrogant intellectualism, his tireless search for meaning, remind one of a latter-day Christian Socrates, probing the corresponding foibles of our political, educational and scientific realms, just as Socrates himself did for ancient Athens. (The parallel between the ancient and the modern thinker is more than fanciful, for Dr. Neumann spent several years in the study of Socrates, the fruits of his labours now being published as *Ueber das Lachen und Studien über den Platonischen Sokrates*, Martinus Nijhoff, The Hague, 1971.)

The teaching of this dialogue is so deep and concentrated that the author has wisely set it out in a seemingly diffuse and broad expanse of talk. Yet even what seem at first reading trivial details have their place in the economy of the argument; and the symmetry of structure which is revealed upon second reading and reflection to the patient student is remarkable. Dr. Neumann has his own 'fifth column' tactic in subverting our cherished prejudices and hallowed misconceptions.

God is Spirit. Man has been created in God's image, and is therefore a spiritual being, capable of decision. Turning away from God to self-love, and worship of his own will, man can only be reached by consummate strategy. God has parachuted his secret agent, conscience, into the very heart of the city of mansoul. Conscience, which is we ourselves, conveys God's call to us. Thus true Omnipotence acts upon man without lifting a finger. For God lets our conscience call us to our real selves and us to himself, in everything that happens to us.

Here is the essence of Frederick Neumann's hermeneutic, applied elsewhere with infinite variation in his sermons. It is always with the human beings of Scripture that our author concerns himself. We see conscience at work in them as they meet natural or human events. In his sermons, Biblical men's and women's experience always points explicitly to Jesus Christ. In the dialogue, a work of apologetic, intended for cultured despisers and apostate theologians, the Christian tone is more implicit, but the ground upon which such Christian application in preaching must rest is laid bare for us to see.

In the dedication to 'God's Fifth Columnist' Frederick Neumann explicitly mentions his debt to Søren Kierkegaard. But there are other voices in whose debt he is. The Blessed Job guides the dialogue to its close. Theologically, it is a meditation on certain teachings of St. Paul. In his exposition of conscience and related topics the impress of John Calvin, among others, is manifest. There is in fact a sense in which 'God's Fifth Columnist' seems a twentieth century counterpart to the existentialist description of faith by Calvin in terms of knowledge of God and knowledge of self. For Frederick Neumann as for John Calvin, the work of conscience is to draw men truly to worship God, not in ritual acts only, but in every thought and deed of their lives.

A word must be said concerning Dr. Neumann's use of the Book of Job. As the dialogue proceeds, he prepares us obliquely for the full and explicit application of Job chs. 38 ff. in Part iv. Deftly turning a thunderstorm, occurring during the final conversation of the two friends, Claimant and Tester, to the question at issue, he shows how storm and conscience lead men to a knowledge of a different order from that of science, a knowledge not intellectual, cumulative, but interpretive, interpretive of man's true nature and true relation to God. This scene culminates in a fragment of high poetry, worthy of Job himself:

> He summons our conscience out of the storm . . .
> Manifesting his majesty,
> And the futility of our self-worship
> And all our foolish claims.

3. Looking Back

Address To Young People

AMONG THE MANY SUBJECTS I have treated in public addresses these thirty years one is conspicuous by its absence: myself. Of the reasons I have for taking restrictions in this respect I will mention two.

The founder of the republic of Czechoslovakia, Thomas G. Masaryk, once granted a series of interviews to a famous writer who was working on his biography. During one of those interviews the writer asked him: 'What did you do, Mr. President, during the 'eighties of the last century?' 'Blunders,' was the reply. This anecdote easily explains why I do not feel particularly inclined to talk about my own life. For then I had to mention many blunders which is not a pleasant affair.

But there is a more serious reason for reticence. I believe all a man has to say is determined and shaped by his personal experiences. Does that make it necessary or desirable to relate one's experiences? By no means. Without a brush you cannot paint a picture, but that does not mean that the brush with which you paint the picture should be in the picture. A man who talks easily about his experiences is like a painter who reproduces a glorious mountain and on top of it puts a picture of his brush. Or again, he portrays a beautiful girl and places on her nose a portrait of his beautiful brush. To *use* one's experiences is one thing, to *present* them is another.

Nevertheless, there are occasions when the latter is permissible. Sometimes, a brush may quite legitimately appear in a picture, for instance a still life. Though it is not a sort of still life I am going to present tonight. I will talk on my experience of conversion. The reason is simply that I have been asked to make a confession of faith, which in this setting is supposed to be given not in a systematic but rather in an experiential way.

So, here is my story: I was born of Jewish parents in the city of Vienna in the last year of the last century. My parents together

11

with an uncle spared no sacrifice to get me an all round high
education. The way I was brought up at home and at school was
not particularly Jewish. It was, what today is called humanistic.
The ideas and ideals that influenced me were moral and cultural
rather than religious. When I was a little boy I believed in God
and, for some time, said my prayers at bedtime, but afterwards
dropped it altogether. At the age of ten I made a religious, or let
me rather say irreligious, experiment of the kind many a boy has
made. I had resolved to settle the question of the existence of
God once and for all. So I said to myself one morning, when I
was on my way to school: 'If I meet my school-mate so and so at
a certain corner I will conclude that there is a God, but if I don't
meet him there is no God'. I did not meet him, so I gave up
believing in God.

Up to the age of seventeen my interests were mainly aesthetical.
Literature, art, music—that was the world in which my mind
moved. I wrote a few poems and felt rather enthusiastic about
them. Then a reaction set in. I became convinced that with all
my aesthetical inebriation I lacked a fundament on which to build.
There was nothing solid in me. My life was all unreal, a mere
shadow. Yet I yearned for reality and substance. My yearning
led me to throw myself passionately into the study of philosophy.
I studied several of the great classical authors. Some of their
tenets attracted me, others repelled me. I made keen use of my
critical faculties and that business engaged my emotions in a
strong measure. During my studies I hit on a thinker who was
not a philosopher in the technical sense, the great Danish Christian
writer, Søren Kierkegaard. Kierkegaard had died in the fifties of
the nineteenth century, yet when I read him I felt myself addressed
by a contemporary. What I met there was not only a seriousness,
a radicalism, an energy and integrity of thought I had not found
elsewhere nor was it the unsurpassed brilliancy of expression. It
was, above all, something authoritative beyond dispute. I do not
refer to instituted authority of a more or less legal character. That
would not have made any impression on me. The authority I
encountered in studying Kierkegaard was one that challenged my
conscience and in doing so proved to be a true and living authority.
As to Kierkegaard, he never claimed authority for himself. He
was quite unambiguous in pointing to the authority of him whose
witness he was: Jesus Christ. So I was brought face to face with

Jesus Christ who demanded my faith, the surrender of my whole being.

Against this surrender I struggled hard and for a long time. I did not and could not talk with anybody about what concerned me most. So I was left to myself yet was never alone—as I understand it now.

I still remember what was perhaps my first personal prayer. I asked God to spare me the awful decision of faith, at least for one year. And really, for about a year, I no longer suffered the continuous haunting of my conscience by the alternative either to yield to Christ or be drowned. After a year, however, that frightful challenge came back, fortified by an increased conviction of sin. I was introduced to myself as one whose presence I could stand no longer. Either I would give my heart to Christ, or I would have to remain all impure, insincere, unreal, the mere shadow of a human being. To this challange I offered the following reply: I declared myself prepared to surrender to Christ if his claim on me could be proved to be true. But could it? Perhaps Jesus Christ was only one out of many religious ideas that had grown within the human mind. What could convince me that a true reality on the other end corresponded to this idea? The Bible? How could it be proved that the Bible contained the true revelation of God? Perhaps it was only a document of human soliloquy. How to decide the issue of truth? By that time I had become clearly persuaded that in matters of faith there was no such thing as an external criterion. Here, you cannot prove anything from experience or observation. Nor can you rely on your own feelings. How then to attain the truth? The question nearly drove me mad.

In the fall of 1918 I studied a book by Kierkegaard which in a heart-grasping manner presented the suffering Christ. Its title is: *Practising Christianity*. The suffering Christ spoke to my condition in an entirely unprecedented manner. Confronted with his appeal, I arrived at my decision. I still remember the place in my room, where I was sitting, the direction from which the light fell, when the following meditation impressed itself on my mind with an irresistible power:

'Forget the question of the authenticity of the Bible, forget everything. Suppose you have just returned from your grocer where you bought some cheese. You unfold the scrap of paper in which the cheese is wrapped and find, written on the paper the following

words: "God became man, died and rose again to save you from
your sins". No doubt this anonymous message lacks the backing
of any outward authority. In order to know what to make of it
you depend entirely on its content. "To save you from your sins"
—that means a life and death question for you. Thus this ugly
scrap of paper presents you with the most serious challenge. But
is it true that God became man, died and rose for me? How to
find out? Suppose for a moment, it is true. In this case God
has determined to leave you without any instrument in your hand
or in your mind with which to settle the question of truth. If that
is so and if God is not a cruel tyrant but really the one who died
for you—then the only conclusion is *that he means you personally
to be the instrument for settling the question of truth.* At present
you are not, but you ought to become. How? *By making yourself fully responsible* for the way you react to the message you just
read. You have to take the message most seriously. You must
realise that now all depends on you. You cannot know anything
before you have made your real decision. Take up your responsibility and you will come to know whether Jesus Christ is real or
not.'

(All depends on your decision. There is no decision against
Christ. The alternative is all between decision and continued
indecision. To invite you to take or to renew this decision was
the purpose of my presentation.)

That brought me around. I could not help making myself
responsible for attaining, or missing, the truth. The moment I did
I was seized with an unshakable conviction of the truth of the
Gospel of Christ. And this conviction has never since left me.
Nor was I ever since in doubt about the nature of the Christian
faith. Faith in Christ is a matter of conscience in a way nothing
else is. In the free, responsible decision of faith the human conscience comes into its own.

A conversion marks a new start but no more. After the event
described I had much to learn and I have still much to learn. I
had not only to change many opinions I held, I had, above all, to
change my life as I still have, day by day. Yet my faith in Christ
has not changed and I firmly hope never will. And certain characteristics of my faith have not changed either.

First of all, I am a Protestant Christian. I was brought to
Christ and not to any self-perpetuating religious tradition. My

decision of faith was a free personal decision, not at all influenced
by the legalistic claims of human authorities.

Second: I came to Christ from far away. That meant an intense
struggle yet it meant, at the same time, being spared many a hard
struggle in which a good number of my Christian friends had to
engage. Since I was not brought up in a Christian tradition, I
never found myself confronted with the necessity to decide between
such issues as, for instance, liberalism versus fundamentalism.
Fundamentalism never meant anything to me but an error. With
the liberals I share their social concern, their discovery that Christian love moves not only through the channels of private charity
but must act on the public level as well, furthermore their freedom
from absolutising and idolising the past and their insistence on an
unmuzzled, scientific investigation of the Bible. At the same time,
I have found much more truth in the classical creeds and Church
doctrines than many of my liberal friends have. I believe, for
instance, in miracles. I believe in a real supernatural. The story
I told you seems to me a rather miraculous one. Generally speaking, I hold that our supreme allegiance and sole worship are due
to God alone and not to our poor ideas of natural law and historical necessity. Yet I am not a fanatic. It is easy for me to enjoy
fellowship with Christians of different opinions. I do not like
Church parties. I am neither a Neo-orthodox nor an Evangelical.
That is to say, I am definitely evangelical but only in the adjectival
connotation of the term. As I resent being labelled I also try not
to label others.

And that makes me feel quite at home in our Congregational
Christian family of Churches. The only 'ism' to which I can
subscribe gladly and without mental reservation is Congregational-
ism with the free and responsible fellowship of Churches it stands
for.

Third: When I came to Christ I came to the suffering Christ.
The love of God, making its supreme sacrifice on our behalf—that
is still the centre of my faith and theological thought. It took me
years after my conversion until I was prepared to join a Church.
That was due to my Jewish background. The differences between
Jew and Jew are no smaller than those between Gentile and Gentile.
Yet every Jew whatever his personal persuasions, knows himself at
the bottom of his heart as a member of a suffering community. He
hates leaving and thus betraying his suffering community. He is

ashamed of it.   Yet I am not ashamed of having left the Synagogue
for the Church.   For the Church of Christ as the New Testament
pictures it, is also a suffering community and that in a deeper and
more productive sense than the Synagogue can be.   To be a
Christian means to be united to the suffering Christ.   Eternal life
as it starts already here on earth, true spiritual life is a resurrection
life.   Before I can rise with Christ I must die to myself over and
over again.   This message which is an integral part of the Gospel
means a stumbling block to the Jew and the Greek in everybody's
heart.   If you proclaim it to others not many will heed your
testimony.   You will meet resistance, active and passive.   That is,
in my view, the permanent meaning of 1 Timothy 3: 12, "All who
desire to live a godly life in Christ Jesus will be persecuted".   That
is true, my friends, though there are many forms of persecution,
some of them rather subtle.   When I left the Synagogue I did not
join a triumphant, imposing ecclesiastical organisation.   What I
joined was and will remain unto the last day a poor little flock,
always in opposition to the world, therefore opposed and scorned
by the world, yet loving a world that opposed and scorned it and
dedicating itself to its service.   It is the Cross that distinguishes
the individual Christian; it is the Cross that distinguishes the body
of Christ, his Church.

   I have talked enough about myself.   Let me close with a little
talking about you, my friends.   I can imagine some well-meaning
person, criticising me for what I said and particularly for the viewpoint under which I said it.   'These are all young people, aren't
they?   And here comes a man, telling them about a suffering
Christ and a suffering Church as if that could in any way concern
them.   Is that a message for young folk?   They do not wish to
anticipate some later sufferings.   They want to live and express
themselves without being bothered with pessimistic apprehensions.'
Now I want to tell you why I consider such an objection entirely
out of place.

   Youth is in one way or the other always driven by a spirit of
opposition.   This spirit sometimes expresses itself in scurillous
ways like disobedience to parents and teachers, silly actions and
so on.   Yet behind all that there is a deeper-seated dissatisfaction.
More recently this dissatisfaction has been subjected to much
psychological research that has brought some valuable results.   I
believe, however, that something more than scientific approach is

necessary in order to understand youth. The real object of your criticism and resentment is, in the last analysis, *the world*, as John in his Gospel uses the term, a world that has turned its back to God. Therefore it has grown so dull and stale and spiritless and sometimes callous. It is here that the picture of the suffering Saviour comes in. What confronts you as an evil of unknown nature and origin the Lord Jesus Christ faced, stood, withstood and overcame. At the cost of his life he exposed himself to the frontal assault of all that you inwardly resent. He was up against the world, suffered from it, died at its hands—yet all that for the sake of the very world that killed him. Thus he has made a reconciliation for which every one of you longs and craves in his heart of heart. Then he was raised from death and entered eternal life to lead us all to where he is. Now when you are grumbling and jeering at older people and conditions produced by them—what are you really doing? You are protesting without knowing that that against which you protest is in you as well as in the world around you. Yet the true meaning of your protest is not negative. It is positive, a profound home-sickness. At the root of all juvenile protest is the hand of God that draws you toward your true destination: eternal life. It is simply not true that young people have no relation to eternal life. In fact, they need not be brought into that relationship. For it is already there, established by the work of God in their hearts. The thing that is demanded of you is to understand the real nature of your inward troubles. Let Christ be your almighty guide to eternal life. Then, only then will you live real lives in this world, standing on firm ground, fighting for good and against evil, within you and without you. You will be at home in God's glorious creation if you realise and express it in your life that your personal goal and the goal of the whole Creation is beyond—from where Jesus Christ in his triumphant love leads all who cling to him, to their eternal home.

4. Luther's Spiritual Development Before the Reformation

MARTIN LUTHER was born at Eisleben, Central Germany, in 1483. His parents sprang from peasant stock. His father, by profession a miner, worked himself up from poverty to a certain measure of wealth, which enabled him to let his gifted son study. Young Luther went to the University of Erfurt where he studied law.

Already as a youth, Luther was concerned for his spiritual welfare. Two personal experiences, the sudden death of his friend and his own narrow escape during a thunderstorm, filled him with a sense of urgency. He resolved to obey the will of God, whilst there was still time left for him—according to the ruling standards of the age, the perfect surrender to God found its clearest expression in choosing the life of a monk. Luther left the University and entered a monastery.

His duties as a monk he took very seriously. Willingly, even passionately he submitted to the strict monastical discipline, and for some time felt quite happy at this way of life. He never longed to return to the world which he had left, nor did he encounter any difficulties in keeping his vow of chastity. When his troubles started, they proved to be of an entirely different kind.

The aim of monastic discipline was to help the monk to live a godly life by keeping him on a kind of middle road between the two extremes of pride on one hand and despair on the other. Luther, however, after some time, began to realise that he could not attain this balanced state of mind. *With him* the scales turned, more and more definitely toward despair. What had happened? Did the monkish life refuse to give him sufficient satisfaction in the long run? That was not his concern. He had not entered the monastery in order to find satisfaction in himself. He had entered it in order to satisfy God and his demands.

Of this, however, he despaired. He became more and more convinced that he did not please God. When he asked himself for the reason, he did not find it with the monastical rules nor with his superiors or fellow-monks, but only with himself. For to Luther, unlike countless other people before and after him, religion meant something quite different from an elaborate method of serving God according to the accepted standards. To him, religion was a matter of his personal conscience. And his conscience was bound by the revealed Word of God in Scripture. He would have to undergo a revolutionary change as to his understanding of Scripture, but its supreme authority had ever stood firm to him. He was a devoted and zealous adherent of the Church of Rome, so long as he believed that its teaching was in accordance with Scripture. When he would realise that this was not the case, he would break with Rome. Yet, to reach this point would cost him ten years of hard, lonely struggles. To these struggles let me now proceed.

Their great theme was in one word: Righteousness. 'How can I, a sinner, satisfy the Holy God's demands?' That was Luther's fundamental question. At the Scripture verse which became most important for the whole history of his life, Romans 1: 17, Luther read that the righteousness of God was revealed in the Gospel. He asked himself how this revelation could make him satisfy God. The answer which he found with the Doctors of the Church was in brief: the righteousness of God is revealed in the Gospel in order to be accomplished by us. This, of course, required the assistance of Divine Grace. But if we only did our bit, Christ would grant us his Grace to let us reach the goal.

And here Luther's troubles started: For what, if a man was, like him, convicted by his conscience that he had not done his bit nor ever did? True, God would not demand of him more than he could do. But did he, *Luther*, really do what he could do? In the presence of the Holy God, Luther had to reply in the negative. Then, however, the Gospel of Christ was of no avail to him. He was unworthy of any Divine support, unworthy of Grace. He was lost.

Or was there still any hope for him? According to the teaching of the Church of Rome, there was a tremendous help in the Sacraments of the Church. It was as if the Church would say to him, her loyal son: 'You are suffering from conscience troubles, I understand. Just leave this to me! If you have sinned, betake yourself to the Sacrament of penitence and you will be restored to

C

full spiritual health'. Luther obeyed and had recourse to the
Sacrament of penitence, but only in order to find his troubles
increased. According to the Doctors, true repentance presupposed
that one loved God. But it was just the cause of Luther's troubles
that he did not love God as he ought to. He realised that his
contribution was always mixed with selfish motives. With a would-
be repentance, however, he could not lay his conscience at rest.
Thus, he came to the conclusion that his repentance did not satisfy
God. To the same conclusion he was led by the practical results.
For whenever he had used the Sacrament as prescribed, confessed
his sins to his Father Confessor and received Absolution, he would
soon have to admit that his state of heart had not changed. He
was still the same sinner as before. For sin meant to Luther not
a mere slip but rather the terrible fact that he did not love God
and his neighbour as he ought to. And this malady could not be
cured by the Sacrament of penitence.

His despair grew and threw him into heavy spiritual temptations.
The righteousness of God as revealed in the Gospel presented
itself to him as a righteousness unto death, even a righteousness
unto Hell. What was the purpose of the Gospel, if God had sent
his Son into this world only in order to become our Judge?

If a man despairs of God, he will quickly despair of himself, too.
From several descriptions of the tempted soul in Luther's later
lectures on the Psalms, one has drawn the inference that for some
time he had been tormented by the thought that he was one of the
reprobates, predestinated to suffer eternal damnation. Then his
temptations must have reached their climax. Luther entered a
very dangerous crisis. At this juncture the unexpected happened.
The most terrible of all challenges was met by Luther with a
blessed, whole-hearted decision of faith. He decided to surrender
unconditionally to the will of the Holy God: If God had destined
him to be lost for ever, he was prepared to suffer it for God's sake.
His will be done. If God wanted him to perish, Luther must
glorify him by perishing. When Luther had thus surrendered himself to God, peace entered his heart, and he knew that God loved
him. His doubts with regard to his election vanished away.
Resignation unto Hell had opened to him the gate of Heaven.
From then on, the figure of the crucified Saviour impressed itself
on his heart. To follow Jesus meant the break-down of his selfish
will. Even his passionate concern for his spiritual welfare had

been tainted by selfishness. Therefore, he had to suffer the mortification of even this desire. In submitting to God's inward spiritual chastisements, he realised that his Heavenly Father was nearest to him when he appeared farthest.

To renounce everything was to gain everything; affliction was the access to joy; mourning brought comfort, despair—hope, poverty—riches. Luther then understood that the great light that shone in the darkness of his soul issued from the Cross of Christ. His share in Christ's sufferings meant his share in the power of his resurrection. Later he could write: 'Our Heavenly Father loves us so passionately, that in his embracing arms we lose the breath of our souls'. The Cross of Christ had become to him all in all.

If we consider this experience from the historical point of view, it proves similar to the one which the great Saints of the medieval Church, from Saint Bernard to Saint Thomas à Kempis, had made and had testified, vigorously, in their writings. Thus, Luther in his lonely struggles was led to a personal appropriation of the treasures of the past.

Yet we must not overlook what seems to me one of the distinctive features of Luther's personality. With him, the devotional and the theological were welded into one. In modern words: Luther led a theological existence. Therefore, his theology was, and still is, so much alive. His personal struggles were closely connected with his undaunted quest for the right approach to the Word of God in Scripture. To these personal needs, vocational duties were added when, after what one might call a splendid career, he was appointed Professor of Theology with the title of a Doctor of the Holy Scriptures in 1512. All the time, his passionate Scripture studies drew their main motive from his initial question: 'How can I, a sinner, come to please God?' He knew that only the Word of God in Scripture could reveal to him the true and certain answer. Yet, over and over again the wrong understanding of the Righteousness of God in Romans 1: 17 barred his way. He besieged this Scripture place like a citadel. He never let loose. Let me quote the words in which he described, later, his long struggle for the truth and his first great victory:

'Should God just use the Gospel in order to add new pains to our old ones, by showing forth his wrath? Thus I asked myself. Raging with the fierce troubles of a perplexed conscience, I yet knocked at that verse in Romans like an inopportune beggar. For

I was driven by a most ardent desire to know what St. Paul meant to say. Days and nights I meditated, until, through the Mercy of God, I grasped the context of the words which runs as follows: "For therein is the Righteousness of God revealed from faith to faith: as it is written: The just shall live by faith".

'Then I realised for the first time that the Righteousness of God was the *gift of God* through which the righteous live by faith. And the meaning of the sentence is, that in the Gospel a Divine Righteousness has been revealed through which God *justifies* us miserable ones by faith: as it is written: "The just shall live by faith". Then I felt myself entirely born again as one who had entered Paradise through an open gate. From then on, my whole outlook on Scripture was changed.'

How was this victory won? By defeat. Luther's former exegesis had to break down in order to make way for the saving knowledge of Grace. The Cross of Christ had to be applied to Luther's exegetical endeavours, too. Man in his pride wants to consider himself righteous before God has made him righteous. It was this attitude, and not any intellectual difficulties, which had veiled to him with darkness Paul's clear statements.

Luther's discovery, though it was new *to him*, was in fact only the recovery of what the greatest theologians of the past had already worked out. For as Luther was soon to learn, Augustine, the strong proclaimer of free Grace, had declared that our righteousness before God consisted in our being made righteous by God in virtue of God's merits. Luther in his own spiritual development, had to recapitulate the chief stages of medieval piety and theology before he made the ultimate step towards the Reformation. Thus, the Reformation kept historical continuity and was, according to the true apostolic succession, provided with its catholic fundament. Yet, Luther dared not stop at this point. Had he done so, he might have stood out as the great renewer of Augustinianism and one of the most revered teachers of the Church of Rome. But God called him to pass beyond Augustine, in order to lead further on. Further, in which direction? Further back to the New Testament.

According to Augustine, God justified the believer by pouring the Holy Spirit into his heart, thus making him a new creature. Justification is, to use the technical term, identical with infusion of Grace.

Now, Luther himself owned a rich experience of the Holy Spirit's renewing power in his heart and life. At the same time, he knew that there was still much left unrenewed with him. For he did not satisfy God's demands completely. He still sinned. If Justification was equivalent to renewal, then he was not completely justified. Then, however, his sins were not forgiven *completely*. He might cherish some hope of being saved in the future, but he was not saved yet. To a man, however, who took the reality of sin as seriously as Luther did, a partial forgiveness was no forgiveness at all. Yet Scripture proclaimed nothing short of total forgiveness, and it also proclaimed a complete Justification as a *present* gift to the believer. Furthermore, Scripture is far from identifying the sinner's justification with the gift of the Holy Spirit.

When Luther realised this, the most refined theories of the schoolmen failed him. Then his eyes were opened as—to our knowledge—no man's eyes had been opened for 1450 years, to what the Apostle Paul really taught in Romans. And this was quite clear and simple teaching. *According to the Apostle, Justification means just as much as acquittal.* God acquits the believing sinner from his guilt and counts him for righteous. For, whenever a sinner puts his trust in Jesus Christ, God does regard the claim of Christ to have died and risen on this sinner's behalf. When Luther understood this, he also understood that the renewing and transforming work of the Holy Spirit *does not precede* the Divine Word of pardon, but *follows* it. To put it again in technical terms: We are saved, not by infusion of Grace, but by imputation of Christ's righteousness to the believer. Luther liked to illustrate the mystery of imputation by employing a beautiful picture, derived from Scripture: Christ is the bridegroom, the believing soul is his bride. Those two are made one. Thus, everything that belongs to the one, belongs to the other as well. *Christ* presents the believer with his righteousness. The believer, for his part, gives Christ his sins. The sin is engulfed in the infinite abyss of Christ's righteousness, which remains immaculate and is thus again presented to the believing soul.

Justification must not be confused with Sanctification, though it issues in Sanctification. Luther never tired to inculcate that faith genders love which brings forth the fruits of love. On the other hand, any human deeds or thoughts which do not spring from the source of faith, must come short of satisfying God. "For whatsoever is not of faith, is sin" (Rom. 14: 23).

Let me sum up what faith meant to Luther. In all his struggles, he had been cast upon *faith*, when his own attempts to come to a solution failed him. When he despaired of being elected, he learned to submit to the will of God—by faith. When he despaired of his own righteousness, he learned to grasp the Divine *gift* of righteousness—by faith. And when he had to admit that even the new life in a regenerate soul was spoiled by the sin which doth so easily beset us—his soul embraced the Heavenly bridegroom, Jesus Christ, by faith *alone*. Thus faith proved to him the only bridge between God and Man. Faith alone establishes fellowship with God. Faith alone makes all Divine gifts available to us. And as the proper Divine gifts are spiritual, contained in his revealed Word, faith proves its all-efficiency by opening up the Word of God in Scripture.

I have come to the close of my sketch. What I told you was a challenge to me when I learned it first, and has never since lost its grasp upon me. It would be foolish to deny the Lord's will and power to lead his Church still further on than was done in the period of the Reformers. We might even be in a great need to be led further, which again means: further back to Scripture. Yet, one thing I know: Unless we first appropriate the treasures of our spiritual inheritance, we shall not make any headway. We might even suffer further weakening. "For whosoever hath, to him shall be given, and he shall have more abundance; but whosoever hath not, from him shall be taken away even that he hath" (Mt. 13: 12).

5. The Dialogue Between God and Man

i. The Concept of God

Exodus 14: 1-31; 15: 20-21.

THE TWO FUNDAMENTAL ASSERTIONS about God in the New Testament are both found in the writings of John: "God is spirit" (Jn. 4: 24) and "God is love" (1 Jn. 4: 16). Both statements are stripped of their entire meaning and significance if they are separated from the context of the Old and New Testament revelation. That little, if anything, remains of them in this case can easily be shown. For the average man today who has no idea of the Bible the statement that God is spirit will convey the idea that he is something like a thin and airy being. The other assertion that God is love must suffer the interpretation that he is rather soft. That is, of course, all absolute nonsense.

The song of Miriam which I just read to you can help us to discover the oldest concept of God in the Hebrew Christian tradition, and one that remains valid and fundamental through the whole Bible. I call it the oldest, because there is no reason to deny that these two lines were composed immediately after the crossing of the lake that divided Egypt from Asia. As to the account of the crossing found in the preceding chapter we cannot make the same statement. It is composed from several sources that date from a period between the tenth and the sixth century B.C. It is not what we, today, understand for history. Only part of it describes the historical events at the close of the Exodus while another represents a powerful and profound theological interpretation of these events. The nucleus of this interpretation is already found in the song of Miriam. In order to understand the concept of God it involves, we must at first try to reconstruct the outlines of the historical occurrences to which it refers.

What the Israelites actually crossed was not the Red Sea. The

25

Hebrew word that has been wrongly translated red sea means sea
or lake of reeds.   It was an inland lake, situated on the eastern
frontier of Egypt, either about thirty miles to the South of the
Mediterranean coast or, as some scholars hold, very near the coast.
When the Israelites approached this shallow lake, part of it was
being dried up by a strong east wind that blew all night, as one of
our sources has it.   With their light equipment the Israelites could
easily cross over.   The pursuing Egyptian army with their great
number of heavy chariots could not move quickly through the
marshes and swamps.   Before they had reached the eastern shore
of the lake the direction of the wind was reversed and a strong gale
brought the waters of the lake back.   Or, if the scene of the events
was laid near the Mediterranean, we might think of a catastrophe
like the one that brought disaster to North Western Europe earlier
this month.   Be this as it may, by the time the Israelites had safely
arrived on the other side of the lake the Egyptian army was prac-
tically annihilated.

Those are all natural events, part of them of a catastrophic
nature.   The song of Miriam, however, sees God at work in those
natural events.   "Sing to the Lord, for he has triumphed gloriously;
the horse and his rider he has thrown into the sea."   The natural
events, described before, are interpreted as caused by the Lord to
whom praise is given for the mighty deliverance of his people from
tyrannical power.

This interpretation is quite in accordance with the name of God
which in our translation is rendered with 'the Lord'.   The Hebrew
word is Jahweh.   About the origin of this name there are various
opinions, but it seems highly probable that Moses and those whom
he taught understood it to mean: 'He who causes to be what comes
to pass', or 'He who causes to happen what happens' (J. Muilen-
burg, *Interpreter's Bible*, I. 301).

This concept of God must not be interpreted in the way of elaborate doctrine or abstract thought.   The later doctrine of God as the
Creator and only Ruler of the whole Universe will in due course of
time evolve from it and so will the faith in the one omnipotent
God.   Moses, however, must have understood the Jahweh name
in very concrete and dynamic terms.   Jahweh, the God of Israel,
is the one with whom we see ourselves permanently confronted;
who deals with us through everything that comes to pass.   In the
words of contemporary Old Testament scholars: 'It is Jahweh

alone who counted for anything and he counted for everything'
(Cuthbert Simpson, *Int. Bible*, I. 444). 'As the God of Israel who
had met this people in a historical event, he thus was recognised
as the Lord of all events who was directing the whole course of
history to his own ends, for nothing happened in either nature or
history in which his power was not acknowledged.' And again:
'God was known in Israel because events were interpreted as his
handiwork' (G. E. Wright, *ibid.* 352 and 353). You see that our
rendering of the name with 'the Lord' following the earliest Jewish
translation into Greek does not sufficiently express the power of
the word. Still there is no better translation except perhaps a
poetical expression I take from a beautiful Church hymn: *Lord of
all being.* Inserting the expression into the song of Miriam, we
might thus render it: 'Sing to the Lord of all being, for he has
triumphed gloriously; the horse and his rider he has thrown into
the sea'.

One cannot accuse the composer of this song of having ignored
or belittled the natural events that made the passage of the Israelites possible and caused the destruction of the Egyptian forces.
Without those happenings to which clear reference is made in the
song this song could never have been composed. They were
definitely in the mind of the composer and singers. The events
that happened were taken for what they were, but their natural
aspect is not the proper theme of the song. The theme of the song
is the glorious Divine action of judgment and redemption. There
is no conflict between the events and their theological interpretation.

For it would be absurd to challenge this interpretation of history
with the objection that it was not God but rather wind and tide
that had brought about the Israelites' deliverance. For the instru-
mentality of wind and water remains undisputed in the song. God
acted through wind and water. The interpretation does not claim
God as just another cause, perhaps a much stronger cause beside
wind and water. As if there were three main factors to distinguish
which in their working together caused the events: the gale, the
tide and also the Lord. The Lord does not move on the same
plane with wind and water.

Nor is it intended to make God a cause behind the visible causes,
only one removed backwards. God has often been designated as
the cause of causes, but never in the Bible. He carries and sur-

rounds the whole chain of causes, therefore cannot be placed within it. God is not like any link in this chain, albeit the first link. The biblical concept of God and the deistic one are diametrically opposed. If God is viewed as the first mover who puts the whole chain of causes into motion like a clockwork, he is not God but a thing. Even if to this thing personality is ascribed it is not Divine personality. For the mere ascription of personality to God does not do justice to the unique causality, if we may call it causality, which the name of Jahweh claims for him. If a boy throws a pebble into a puddle we may say that the event caused has been caused by a person. Yet the way it was caused is not personal but mechanical, at all events it remains within the causal nexus. The God of the Bible, however, absolutely transcends the whole nexus and his actions are never mechanical but personal throughout.

This statement needs further elaboration and clarification. Let me use an illustration. If a man throws a pebble into a pool of water, we can make the following distinctions, proceeding from the events caused backwards through the chain of causes.

1. The event caused is the stirring of the waves in the pool.

2. What caused the event was the act of throwing a pebble in a certain direction.

3. What flung the pebble through the air was a man's hand.

4. The cause of the motion of the man's hand was a cerebral process.

And now you are at liberty to supply further causes, physiological, psychological, sociological ones, depending on the view you take of the nature of motivation.

Now let me interpret the *same* event theologically, that is, as a Divine action. We shall state, then, that God caused the stirring of the waves in the pool. This statement does not, however, eliminate any of the causes enumerated or suggested before. All my former statements remain untouched. Nor are we now concerned with the often discussed problem as to whether the pebble-throwing man acted spontaneously or involuntarily, whether or not he was free, totally or partially, to throw the pebble, and if he was free, what the meaning of his freedom should be, and so on. All these questions we can disregard so far as our present purpose is concerned. We simply state that the man who throws the pebble into the pool so that its waves are stirred does it as God's instrument. In order now to describe the Divine causality we must make one step further backwards. From the man who throws the pebble and from all possible causes and motives behind his action we must go back to God who causes to happen what happens. I said, we must make one step back, one only. For between God who acts through that whole chain of causes and the chain of causes itself there are no further links interposed. God has no hands to push the man, and further back there is no psychological causation that determines this specific Divine action. God is perfectly free, and in his perfect freedom he works immediately, directly upon that man, respectively the whole chain of causes and motives. There is nothing that could separate God from the sphere of any of his actions. Therefore, in maintaining the Divine causation of this and all events, we must always remain conscious that this use of the term causation and causality is improper, metaphorical.

Using pictorial language we may say that God, having no hands, the man throwing the pebble into the pool functions as his hands. Of course, this picture must not be stressed. One must not think of a relation like that between brain and hand. For between brain and hand there are numerous physiological agencies at work, nerves, sinews, muscles, etc. Nothing of this kind comes into consideration. There is nothing between God who stirs the waves through a man and the man himself.

All this may sound rather enigmatic. On the one hand, the Divine causality is asserted, on the other hand every kind of causality we know from what we call experience is denied to him. Can there no more be said about the power of God who causes everything without being himself a cause? Or to put the question differently: How is it that God acts without entering the sphere of his actions?

Does the Bible furnish us with material for answering this question? I think it does. Let me first remind you of the account of Creation in the first chapter of the book of Genesis. There, the vehicle of the Divine creative power is described under the figure of the Word of God. "And God said, 'Let there be light'; and there was light." The force of this great statement is brought out majestically in the Thirty-third Psalm: "For he spoke, and it came to be; he commanded, and it stood fast" (v. 9). At other places in the Old Testament the Word of God appears as the instrument not only of his creative but also of all other Divine actions. (For instance Ps. 145: 15 ff.) To make the Word the carrier of Divine deeds means to describe these deeds as spiritual ones. For the word is not conceived, here, as the uttering of a sound, *flatus vocis*, but rather as the expression of a personal will, an outgoing of the spirit. Let us make a further step, again directed by an Old Testament text.

We read in the book of Job, 36: 5: "Behold, God is mighty, and does not despise any; he is mighty in strength of understanding". This verse points to the source and essence of Divine power. How can God do everything he wants to do? The answer is: Because he understands everything. Understanding is much more than a mere know-how or even a superb skill. Since the opposite term is: to despise, the word understanding denotes warmth of sympathy and even more than that. God surrounds everybody and everything completely, not with a cold knowledge but rather in virtue of an unfathomable spiritual depth which is the core of all reality (cp. Ps. 139). He understands, he gets to the bottom of everything, he carries everything with his understanding. The Divine strength of understanding is, indeed, the pillar of the concept of a personal God which puts this concept far above an anthropomorphical symbol. To believe in God means, first of all, to believe him who understands me completely as he understands everything completely and who always acts in strength of his understanding.

God is 'mighty in strength of understanding'. I quoted this verse from the American Revised Standard Version though I personally prefer a more literal rendering of the original Hebrew, following the Septuagint and Luther's original translation which was, however, changed by later revisers of the German Bible, much to my regret. The original Hebrew is *kabbir côah lebh*. The Septuagint Greek has *dynatos ischui kardias*, Luther's German: *maechtig von Kraft des Herzens*. The English equivalent would run: God is *mighty in strength of heart*. To me that means the most profound statement the Old Testament makes about the Divine resources, the root and essence of the omnipotent God. All the Divine power derives from the strength of his heart. And the heart of God must not be distinguished from anything else in God. For there is nothing else. The Hebrew word for heart denotes the centre of vitality, the seat of thought, the will and imagination, the hidden inwardness that matters. If we wish to translate the New Testament assertion that God is spirit into Old Testament conceptual language we should have to say that God is all heart. And the direction in which the Divine heart must be ultimately understood is indicated, impressively, in the words which form the inscription over the story of the Exodus: "I have seen the affliction of my people who are in Egypt, and I have heard their cry because of their taskmasters; *I know* their sufferings, and I have come down *to deliver them*" (3: 7-8).

God is all heart. At the bottom of everything that is and happens there is the throb of the Divine heart. And that Divine heart is the heart of the Saviour. From here let us return to what I said about the word of God.

God has created the world and rules it through his word. Everything God has done has the structure and character of the word. If the power to speak his almighty word is the power of God's heart, then all his dealing with us must be interpreted as acts of Divine self-communication. Whatever happens to us as individuals or groups, smaller or larger, manifests God in his concern for us. In everything he causes to happen he goes out to address us personally. God speaks to us continuously. His word is, according to the most radical and profound meaning of the term, the vehicle of his spiritual self-impartation to us. God gives himself to us in his word. And this is not an action intended to remain one-sided.

God is high above us beyond all measure. He transcends everything we can think or imagine. If, however, God is all heart, then the transcendence of God is, in the ultimate issue, *the transcendence of his heart*. God would not speak to us people if he were not inconceivably humble of heart. In virtue of the same unfathomable humility God does not only address us, but also expects and calls forth our answer. Every Divine action is intended to evoke our response. With other words: From the cradle to the grave man is engaged in a continuous dialogue with God. We may know little of it, we may even deny it, but that does not alter the fact. For our refusal to answer God who speaks to us is *also* an answer, though a negative one. Whether we admit it or not, we have our places assigned to us in the Divine-human dialogue which forms the positive meaning of the history of the individuals and nations.

How can man properly respond to God's call?

Certainly not unaided. Human history, as it has actually developed, is the history of man's constantly recurring alienation from God, his wrong-doing and wrong-thinking. Therefore we do not listen to the Divine voice. To save us from ourselves God has revealed himself in the history of the people of Israel. There he has furnished our conscience with a universal pattern for the interpretation of his dealing with us and his Divinely taught interpretation of his actions which is identical with our proper response to them. Apart from our actual answer to the voice of God in his doings, his doings can never be understood. Conversely, our right response is already the sufficient understanding of the ways of God so far as we are concerned, and no more is required from us. For God does not humble himself and speak to us in order to occasion our intellectual exercises. He speaks his heart to us, and that in a matter of facts. He expects us to speak our hearts to him, and that, too, in a matter of facts.

When Israel was delivered from the pursuing Egyptians the people, represented by their women, responded to Jahweh's redeeming action with sacred dance and sung words of praise. In making their response, they understood that it was Jahweh who through the agency of natural events had saved them from their enemies. The theological interpretation of the events cannot for a moment be separated from the act of worship in which the people acknowledged the true meaning of the events. I say *true* meaning, for truth, the truth about God is accessible only through actual worship. Due response and interpretation are one and the same thing. Worship is the responsive action of the heart, and the understanding of him to whom worship is directed can never be divorced from one another. Unless we occupy the place where God wants to meet us we can never meet him. "In thy light do we see light" (Ps. 36: 9).

It is a truism to state that the worship of God which constitutes our answer to his calling us does not exhaust itself in hymn-singing. Shortly after the passing of the sea of reeds the conscience of Israel was given a definite pattern of the knowledge of God in a worshipful life. The great and unique document of this Divine Revelation are the Ten Commandments.

The key to the Ten Commandments is the inscription: "I am the

Lord your God who brought you out of the land of Egypt, out of the house of bondage".

That is the fundamental fact to which the whole of Israel's subsequent history looks back. How to live facing this fact? How to live in the dynamic presence of the Saviour God? How to respond to his work?

The answer supplied by the following, individual commandments is very realistic. It presupposes that the moment God appears on our horizon we are prone to escape from his presence. We know that we owe him all worship; instead we worship something else. "You shall have no other god beside me." One way to escape seems now closed. The human rebellion tries another. We declare ourselves quite willing to worship God, yet stealthily substitute a picture of him that suits our taste better than reality . . . "You shall not make yourself a graven image, or any likeness . . . you shall not bow to them or serve them".

Our futile images stand condemned. Human deceitfulness looks for another method of dodging response. God is acknowledged and worshipped nominally, but only to use him as a means to accomplish our own selfish ends: "You shall not take the name of the Lord in vain".

'All right,' we reply; then throw ourselves on our daily duties and the pursuit of our special interests in order to forget God. Again a forceful reminder intervenes to start us back in the right direction: "Remember the sabbath day to keep it holy".

Suppose we congratulate ourselves on striving, earnestly, to do all those commandments. Immediately the question arises whether our daily lives as we actually live them express our being confronted with the Saviour God. If that were the case we would take full consideration of him whom God has saved along with us, our neighbour. Our relations to our neighbour are shaped by our behaviour in the family. The fundament of the family life is piety: "Honour your father and your mother".

Then in the wider circles in which we move our actions are expressive of the saving Divine presence only if we keep engaged in a permanent fight with those evil impulses that cause us to raise ourselves above our neighbour with our deeds, words or thoughts; to make us lords over his life, his spouse, his property, his honour: "You shall not kill. You shall not commit adultery. You shall

not steal.   You shall not bear false witness against your neighbour.
You shall not covet".

The negative formulation of all but one of the Ten Commandments indicates the struggle in which we must persist in order to
make proper response to God in every situation in which he meets
us and through which he addresses us.   A positive expression of
the gist of the Ten Commandments is represented by the New Testament combination of the two love commandments: "You shall
love the Lord your God with all your heart, and with all your soul,
and with all your mind . . . You shall love your neighbour as yourself" (Mt. 22: 37, 39).

That can never be reduced to what is commonly called ethics.
If you remove the Divine Commandments from the Biblical context, if you rob them of their character as a pattern of human
response to the mighty acts of God that shape our own lives and
the whole of history—you may still preach love, you may earnestly
endeavour to practise it, yet what you take for love will have very
little in common with the understanding of this cardinal term in the
Judaeo-Christian tradition.   You may be a very nice and decent
fellow and a useful member of the community, you will certainly
remain an instrument in the hand of God, but only a blind instrument that does not realise the meaning and purpose of its existence.
For so long as you keep your ears closed to the Divine message, so
long as you refuse to *act upon* the Divine message that challenges
you everywhere—the whole world will be no more to you than the
displays in the windows of a rich store at which you are gazing
from the street without ever taking the decisive step of entering the
store.   And your life will ultimately be marked as that of a
deserter from the human situation and the Divine-human cause it
embodies.   No social concern however profound and passionate
can make good for this betrayal of humanity.

The Biblical Revelation leads us to become aware of the human
situation and take our stand in it.   Through everything that comes
to pass God claims our heart and the factual expression of the
worship of our heart in this particular situation.   He does not,
however, claim our achieving a penetrating analysis of the motives,
the content, the purpose of any of his particular actions.   We can
see the work of the Lord, but we can never see through it.   Why
God in the Exodus events treated the Israelites in one way, the
Egyptians in another can never be explained.   His dealings with us

remain shrouded in mystery. Cheap or primitive explanations can easily be offered, but a consistent, personal awareness of the Biblical Revelation will in the end play havoc with them. Just one illustration: The statement that all of God's doings are his self-disclosures is given its ultimate radical meaning in the book of the prophet Ezekiel. This great prophet extends the revelatory understanding of the Divine actions to the godless and wicked. Let me quote from his prophecy of doom about the haughty prince of Tyre: "Will you still say, 'I am a God', *in the presence of those who slay you*, though you are but a man, and no god, in the hands of those who wound you?" (28: 9). This is but a special application of Ezekiel's standard message: "And they shall know that I am the Lord". This message has in my opinion guided the priestly authors of the latest strands of the Exodus story. In Ezekiel's words against the prince of Tyre the Divine judgment is proclaimed, sternly and unequivocally. Yet the prophet's understanding of the Divine judgment as *revelatory* clearly transcends the primitive view of it as a retributive punishment. Furthermore, the phrase: "And they shall know that I am the Lord", serves likewise to interpret the Divine actions of Grace. The ultimate aim of Grace and Judgment is the same, everywhere. Yet the methods applied differ radically.

Can we understand God? Yes we can, by doing his commandments. If we apply his universal love-commandment to any single situation, then, we understand why God has brought us into this situation. For every Divine action that concerns us is already a reaction. In shaping this particular situation in which I find myself, now, God has taken consideration of my previous answer or refusal to answer. For he understands me and acts upon his understanding. And as he deals with me, he deals with everybody else, at the same time, co-ordinating, creatively and marvellously, all our different situations. If I now act as he wants me to act, I prove that I have understood him. There is no other way of understanding God; this one, if being practised, will give us enough to do and to think, so long as we are here on earth. For God is love and nothing but love can understand love.

ii. Supernatural Freedom
Deut. 11: 1-5, 7; Jn. 10: 34-36; 2 Cor. 5: 17

WE SOMETIMES SAY about certain people that we have nothing
to do with them. They are not our concern. Statements to this
or a similar effect may be justified or not, depending on how they
are meant. They may, for instance, rightly disclaim a certain
brazen interest in the private life of public functionaries and their
wives. On other occasions they may serve as mere excuses for a
callous indifference. There is, however, one case in which no such
disclaimer can be made under any circumstances whatever. For
with God we have always to do. He is and remains our chief
concern—not so much in the moralistic interpretation that he ought
to be. He is. The statement that we have always to do with him
is not primarily imperative. It is indicative. It testifies a fact,
indeed, the most important and inescapable of all facts. With
God we are confronted everywhere. He is active in shaping the
things and events that form the actual situation of any man at any
time. He is no less active in forming the inside of our situation,
the challenges presented to everybody by his actual disposition and
state of mind at any time.

The all-effectual Divine 'Causality' that posits, carries and rules
everything is a spiritual causality. The power God exercises in
creating the Universe and acting on it, continuously, is not the
robust force of wind, earthquake and fire. It rather resides in the
still small voice in which his heart expresses and communicates
itself. This still small voice may use wind, earthquake and fire as
its forerunners. Even so the terrific Divine energy that impinges
on us and the whole Creation derives directly from the holy concern of his humble love for all and sundry. It is this concern,
couched in a language we need to hear.

In his humble love toward us people God has engaged every
human being in a life-long dialogue with him. He addresses us
with the facts and events we experience. He then listens to our
reply and takes it into consideration in working out his rejoinder.

All the works of God are profoundly mysterious, unattainable
to our intellectual grasp. And yet everything he does is a word
by means of which he makes himself known to us. The knowledge
of himself which God offers to us with his action is not the detached
knowledge of the theoretical approach. The knowing response for

which he seeks to prepare us through his factual language is one of worship and worshipful life. We understand the hidden God if we worship him from our hearts and express our worship in actions that are patterned according to his revealed universal love command. This is the positive reply he seeks to draw out from us by lifting us to the position of his partners in a dialogue that forms the essence and the meaning of all history, individual and general.

Within the frame of this dialogue human freedom has its proper place. We are free, here and now, to answer him who addresses us, here and now. In calling forth our reply God sets us free. The uncontradictable effectiveness of the Divine operations that make and surround us is so far from fettering our spirit that, on the contrary, it provides freedom with its setting, its inner possibility, its reality, its meaning.

It prevents us, however, from looking for the locale of freedom in any other context than the one indicated. Freedom solely means freedom to give one's heart to God in offering him the response which he elicits with everything he causes to happen to us. We are free, that is, we are set free, time and again, either to worship God or to refuse him worship. The locale of freedom is the dialogue between God and man.

I am well aware that there are other possible concepts of freedom. One may, for instance, try to state the case for metaphysical freedom in working out its qualitatively different expressions in the various realms of being. One may draw certain conclusions from the unpredictability of the behaviour of individual atoms, from the spontaneity that characterises all organic life, from human self-determination. Different from the metaphysical approach though by no means unrelated to it is the ethical treatment of freedom. You may, for instance, inquire into the relationship of freedom and responsibility and the mysterious operations of conscience. Furthermore, there are certain ideas of freedom that form the conscious or unconscious presuppositions of sciences like history, sociology and psychology. The same may be said of applied sciences. Psychotherapy, for instance, has it as its proper aim to help the patient recover his partially impaired freedom.

Yet all this is beyond the scope of this paper. I consider it a necessary endeavour to unravel the relationship between theological freedom (with which I am dealing exclusively, here) and its natural that is metaphysical-ethical prefigurations (foreshadowings).

I believe, however, that before a clear concept of theological freedom is worked out any attempt like the one indicated would only make for increasing the present confusion. Let me, therefore, in sticking to my present purpose, further pursue the line drawn.

God, in addressing us with everything he causes to be, places us in a vis-à-vis position toward him. The call he extends to us through our actual situation grants us freedom to be used by us in this actual situation. Apart from his call there is no freedom in our relation to God which means *in reality*. I cannot even move a finger without acting as God's instrument. It is all his working. But in doing any of his works that concern me, God has already taken my previous answer to him into consideration. So the Divine action that challenges me now reflects in its content my previous spiritual action in replying to his former manifestation. God calls me. I answer this way or that. In his rejoinder God calls me again. This ever on-going dialogue is one between the Divine and the human heart. For God acts from his heart, and we are free, strictly speaking only in our heart's reaction.

These are not speculative thoughts. In conceiving them and in working them out I have drawn from the only source I know for dealing with the subject, God and man. Let me now proceed to an explicit demonstration of what was implied in all I have said. Let me show it to you from Scripture.

The apostle Paul in his sketch of the apostasy of the pagan world with which the theological argument of the letter to the Romans starts, makes the bold if not to say offensive statement that human vice and wickedness are due to Divinely caused hardening: "God gave them up to a base mind and to improper conduct. They were filled with all manner of wickedness, evil, covetousness, malice. Full of envy, murder, strife, deceit, malignity, they are gossips, slanderers, haters of God, insolent . . . foolish, faithless, heartless, ruthless" (Rom. 1: 28b-31). All this because "God gave them up to a base mind and improper conduct".

No doubt this statement is more radical than the often discussed story of Pharaoh's hardening. It is even more radical than Isaiah 45: 7. Only Ezekiel 20: 25-26 matches it—perhaps.

Is man only a puppet in the hands of a Divine wire-puller? Is God responsible for our evil thoughts and deeds? 'By no means,' Paul would reply, and that quite consistently. Let me read to you the words preceding the ones I just quoted. "And since they did not see fit to acknowledge God, God gave them up to a base mind and to improper conduct" (v. 28). That their actual hardening of mind was the Divinely caused consequence of their own evil decision made at a juncture when they were free to acknowledge the truth but did not see fit to do it—is brought out still clearer in the beginning of the section: "So they are without excuse: for although they knew God they did not honour him as God or give thanks to him, but they became futile in their thinking, and their senseless minds were darkened" (v. 21). They are without excuse, for they had been free either to worship God or to refuse him worship. How did they receive their freedom of decision? Through Divine self-communication. "God has shown it to them" the apostle declares (v. 19). "Ever since the creation of the world his invisible nature, namely his eternal power and deity, has been clearly perceived in the things that have been made" (v. 20). The grandeur and majesty of the Creator was brought home to them by his works. Yet instead of offering him the response of true worship "They suppressed the truth by their wickedness" (v. 18) therefore God gave them up. The darkening and hardening of the human mind is thus understood as the Divine reaction to man's abuse of his freedom. That this hardening serves a Divine purpose beyond itself we shall hear later.

Let me now turn to a very different text. I do this with the purpose to show that the same concept of freedom is presupposed in strands of the New Testament literature that differ widely as to historical background, pictorial and conceptual forms used, situational purpose, trend and direction of thoughts. I refer to the great eschatological discourse in all the synoptical Gospels which has been called 'the little apocalypse'. In this discourse Christ predicts the destruction of Jerusalem, setting it against the background of the end of the world. Both events, the fall of the holy city and the end, are so closely seen together that it seems impossible to separate the respective utterances. Now the history of the end as foretold in this strong and weighty address does not furnish us with a kind of supernatural appendix, added artificially to ordinary history. It is ordinary history, understood radically as facing the end. Therefore all human callousness, all the sufferings of the righteous appear as it were in concentrated form in the concluding chapter of history which only reveals, clearly and unmistakably, what every previous chapter essentially was. One striking feature in this discourse is the announcement that before the final blow will fall upon barren, hypocritical Jerusalem and lawless humanity respectively, "This Gospel of the kingdom will be preached throughout the whole world as a testimony to all nations: and then the end will come" (Mt. 24: 14. Cp. Mk. 13: 10. Lk. 21: 13 has instead: "This will be a time for you to bear testimony"). Through the world-wide preaching of the Gospel as a testimony a last opportunity will be granted to everybody: a time-span of freedom. Then the end will come and with it the judgment according to the use every one has made of his freedom.

In this text freedom is mediated through the preaching of the Gospel rather than God's universal matter of fact language. With the relation of those two vehicles of freedom I shall deal in a short time. Both adduced texts, the one from Matthew as well as the other from Romans, show clearly that freedom is given to us for our actual response to God's call. The moment we have made our decision we are bound to it. Our subsequent actions are gathered up in the Divine rejoinder to our reply. We are in the grasp of necessity. If our reply was positive, worshipful, loving, our subsequent actions must be called free in a wider interpretation of the term. For every human action that results from and expresses a proper spiritual response to God manifests both, the all effective will of God and my own free decision to obey him. It is Divinely shaped and free at the same time. As John says in his Gospel: "He who does what is true comes to light, that it may be clearly seen that his deeds have been wrought in God" (3: 21). Here, freedom is predicated of such human actions as are wrought *in God*. These Divine-human deeds demonstrate God at work. They are positive testimonies to him.

In quite a different sense it can be said that also those human actions that result from lack of freedom due to hardening are revelatory. The act of disobedience is deeply hidden in the heart. In a way it is deeper hidden than the act of obedience. For it belongs to the nature of disobedience to hide. God, however, in hardening the heart of him who resists his call, makes him do the foolish things that reveal the secrets of his heart. He publishes his inner state. He leads his treachery into its absurd consequences. Spiritually speaking, the wicked things the man is doing now are no more foolish and wicked than what he did when he betrayed God secretly in his heart. The outbreak of his terrible illness may give him the only opportunity that can now be offered to him to realise what he did when he disobeyed God in his heart. God continues to call even the hardened man: he calls him through the evil deeds the man is doing.   The man is thus set free to repent. Whatever use he may make of his freedom now, in any case the rebel against God must serve God as a witness to himself and to others to reveal the true nature of the human rebellion.   God deals with every individual and again with every community whatever their attitude to him may be, positive or negative, in the manner formulated by Christ in all the synoptic Gospels: "There is nothing hid except to be made manifest; nor is anything secret except to come to light" (Mk. 4: 22. Cp. Mt. 10: 26; Lk. 8: 17; 12: 2). This is the 'Law' that governs human history from the beginning to the end.

According to the Biblical view of man's spiritual conditions the beginning of history is marked by a fall that has ever since recurred in the history of every individual and of every group, smaller or larger.   Original sin forms an integral part of the spiritual frame of reference given to us for judging ourselves, individually and collectively, in the presence of God.   Throughout the whole of history it forms the starting point from which return to God must be made. The continuous dialogue between God and man cannot be honestly conceived wthout taking original sin into duly serious account. In calling us through the vicissitudes of life, God has already considered our fatal alienation from him.   Every Divine call is a call back, a call to return to him.   About the ultimate results of God's calling every man back to himself, from the stone age down to the present day—we have no statistics and can make no statements. In every pagan religion glimpses of truth and dark spots of falsehood are found together.   Nobody who is not a complete fool will dare to make an estimate about the percentile relation of those who let themselves be led by the sparks of truth to the others who preferred falsehood.   In this connection I want to refer to a very remarkable fact.   The wisest of all men of whom we know outside the Hebrew-Christian tradition, Socrates, used to say of himself: 'I know that I do not know'.   This statement is not tantamount to an acknowledgement of theoretical ignorance.   To Socrates, not to know, was a frightful thing.   The horizon against which Socrates' testimony must be set is what we, today, would call existential if we understand this term in its true, original interpretation by Søren Kierkegaard, disregarding later usurpers who have met with a punishment just the opposite of King Midas'. Socrates' testimony of existential ignorance is the pagan counterpart to the great confessional statement by the apostle Paul in Romans 7: 15, "For that which I do, I know not: for not what I would, that do I practise; but what I hate, that I do".

While God is calling us, we are resisting him and deafening our ears to his call—so long as we prefer to deceive ourselves. So long as we resist him we forfeit the gift of freedom offered to us by his call. In order to reveal that and to arouse our conscience with a strong appeal to return to him, God has made himself known in a particular manner in the history of the people of Israel and through it to all mankind. The depositories of his revelation and the unique testimony to it are the books of the Bible. During the last 200 years we have learned, slowly, to set every Biblical text against its historical background so far as we can reconstruct it. The result is a sharpened understanding of the situational character of the Divine revelation which can help us greatly in its theological and devotional appropriation. No text in the Bible has ever been intended to be looked at as a separate entity, enthroned in the clouds, to which one should or could relate himself, apart from his actual life-situation, present or responsibly anticipated. Every Biblical text is to serve us as it served its original receivers as a help interpreting God's historical dealings with us by bringing him the worshipful response he seeks. Moses and the prophets, the priests, the sacred law-makers, narrators, poets and sages, all of them, including John the Baptist and Jesus as a teacher were proclaimers and renewers of the Divine Law, understood not as a statutory code, a sum of precepts, but rather as a personal Divine exhortation and encouragement to read "the signs of the times" (Mt. 16: 3) in events experienced or foretold. Since God is the same today as he was yesterday and since man's nature has not changed either, the messages of the Bible will remain topical up to the end of the world. Every Scripture message, understood as 'Law', refers to an actual situation present or authoritatively anticipated and interprets it as the wooing of God for the heart of man. It arouses and informs our conscience; it adds power to the voice of conscience; it thus restores our forfeited freedom.

The trite argument offered by Pelagius and later by Erasmus and countless others that the Divine commandments presuppose our freedom—for how could God give us a command unless we were in a position to keep it?—is not only frivolously shallow but also completely out of place from the historical point of view. It fails to realise what a tremendously effective agency the word was to the ancient world. To the ancients the word worked *ex opere operato*, crushing every resistance, 'ignoring' and overruling those with whom it dealt whatever their attitude to it may be. From those very old ideas the Hebrews took the conceptual forms in order to state the fact that when God speaks to us in his revelation he makes out of worms his free partners in a dialogue. Jesus had no use for dynamistic conceptual forms. He traced the whole power of the word of God back to its speaker. In his understanding the effectiveness of the word of God is radical and complete in a measure never realised before. "If he called them gods to whom the word of God came . . ." (Jn. 10: 35. Revelation means Divine self-impartation.

The word of God spoken to man does not presuppose his freedom but restores it to him. It grants us a new opportunity to listen and respond to God's situational call. As this latter has already the structure of the word, the word of God proper represents the essence, the meaning and purpose of all his dealings with us.

What was Israel's attitude to the authoritative interpretation of the word-acts of God offered by the word in its concentrated form? Did they respond to the voice that was now fortified by the loudspeaker of the Law? The ones did, others did not. As to the numbers involved on each side we have no statistics. God alone knows the heart. One thing, however, can be said. Those who obeyed God and whose inner life is documented in the testimonies they left us, realised to a greater or smaller degree how weak, how ambiguous, how self-contradictory their obedience was. In identifying themselves with their people, they cried to God for forgiveness. In answer to their prayers some of them were given the firm hope for an ultimate deliverance of the people from its deep-seated sinfulness. They trusted that after using very stern language, God would lead a faithful remnant to return to him. He would pour his Spirit into their hearts. He would make everything new.

Had the word of God been unable to restore man his freedom? The Israelites received freedom but were brought to realise that the best use they made of it did not do justice to the Divine intention in calling them. They realised their need of being made new. Thus the Law of God revealed to man the most hidden and yet the most monstrous fact about him; that in order to obey God he must be wiped out, then be made over entirely. For God, in revealing himself to man, also reveals man to man. Left to ourselves we know as little about ourselves as we know about God.

God gave his word to Israel and all mankind that we all should from our reaction to his word come to know what is in us. Paul says in Romans that the "Law came in to increase the trespass" (5: 20) and in the seventh chapter he describes the terrible outburst of our hidden rebellion against God the moment he speaks his commandment to us. "When the commandment came, sin revived and I died" (7: 9b). This experience is made by all who strive passionately to obey God. The Law sets them free to obey, but then sin proves stronger than freedom. The fact is as horrible as it is mysterious. We may give it a more positive formulation in stating that the Old Testament revelation is not the ultimate but only the penultimate communication of the love of God to sinful humanity. The last word of the Old Testament saints, the spiritual result of Israel's education through the Law, is the fervent prayer of a broken and contrite heart for the definite and ultimate word to be spoken by God.

In the light of God's ultimate communication to us which is called the Gospel or the New Testament the kind of freedom that I tried to describe until now is not counted deserving the name of freedom. The new wine refuses to be poured into the old vessels. A very strong testimony to this effect is represented by Christ's words to people whom John calls 'the Jews'. John uses this theological term in order to denote the highest degree of human conformity to the will of God so far as his will can be made out from a written code without the aid of the prophetic spirit: "Again Jesus spoke to them, saying, 'I am the light of the world; he who follows me will not walk in darkness, but will have the light of life'. . . . Jesus then said to the Jews who had believed in him, 'If you continue in my word, you are truly my disciples and you will know the truth, and *the truth will make you free* . . . Truly, truly I say to you, every one who commits sin is a slave to sin. The slave does not continue in the house for ever; the son continues for ever. So if the Son makes you free, you will be free indeed" (Jn. 8: 12, 31-32, 34-36).

"The truth will make you free." Also here, freedom is taught to be mediated by the word of God, his spiritual self-impartation. The astonishing thing is that after all we have heard freedom now appears as entirely relegated to the future. "The truth *will* make you free." Freedom is seen solely as the subject of a Divine promise. This implies the denial of present freedom, a denial far more radical than any deterministic philosopher or naturalistic barbarian has ever been able to formulate it. No wonder that Christ's audience was roused to fury—by his promise.

This astonishing reinterpretation of the concept of freedom is entirely the work of Jesus. 'Jesus alone.' He stands quite apart already as a teacher. For although his teaching conveys the word of God in the Old Testament interpretation of the term, it points, at the same time, far beyond it. It points to Christ's death-and-life-work. For Jesus Christ gathered up all he was and had been commissioned to do, in the two Divine-human deeds which in their indissoluble connection form his proper work: his death and his resurrection.

If I should express what the work of Jesus Christ, therefore Jesus Christ himself, means, I would use the Pauline expression of a new Creation. Christ died and rose again in obedient, loving self-identification with us. He died and rose again that we might die and rise with him. In virtue of our death-and-life communion with him which Paul calls faith our old nature with its incorrigible revolt against God is morally destroyed and we are made new to become immortal bearers of the Spirit of Christ, the Spirit of God. "And where the Spirit of the Lord is, there is freedom," Paul declares (2 Cor. 3: 17).

The freedom to decide for or against Christ is a gift of God, mediated through his word and Spirit. For the Gospel, the good news about Jesus Christ interpreted by his Spirit, reaches into the centre of our being, where we can really say to God 'Yes' or 'No'. I say, interpreted by his Spirit. What the work of Christ is all about we must be told in plain words, but these words will touch our inmost being and be really understood only through the home-bringing power of the Spirit of Christ. On the Cross Christ has come so near to us all that he is morally and therefore really in a position to reach our conscience with his Spirit who is the proper Speaker of the Gospel. Apart from the word the Spirit does not speak. Apart from the Spirit the word is not spoken—to me.

The only subject and content of the Gospel is Jesus Christ. Jesus Christ who has accomplished the renewal of fallen man is all God has to say to us. He is God's all-embracing, all availing Yes to man (2 Cor. 1: 20). Jesus Christ is the Word of God in its comprehensive and absolute meaning. He is the whole of the Divine revelation. The one word that the Spirit of God speaks to us is Jesus Christ.

How does the Spirit's Gospel bring about my freedom of decision?

God demands only one thing of me: Love. The death of Christ for me, its reality, its necessity convince my conscience that in order to live for God and my neighbour I must first die to myself. For if Christ died for me he died through me. I did with him and I still do with him what I did and do with God's continuous call and with his word of revelation. Freedom given to me by God's situational manifestations, freedom restored to me by his interpreting word has been of no avail to me. Freedom, entering the scene in order to disappear and be counted for nothing: God's self-impartation to me effaced by my sin—how could it be otherwise if I killed the Son of God who is the Word of God? In the light of the Cross the Spirit brings my conscience to realise that there is no other help left for me except to die and be made new. What the Law through its clash with my sin predicted has been fulfilled by Jesus Christ. He died for me on the Cross—so I am dead. The resurrection of Christ for me, its reality (God is God), its necessity (Christ is God's Yes) convince my conscience that the same overwhelming justice and power that confronts me in every hour of my life has carried the dying Saviour to the attainment of his whole aim. As he lives I live also—in virtue of the self-sacrificing, omnipotent Love of God that gives itself to me in Jesus Christ.

Through the seal the Spirit of truth puts on the Gospel message I am granted freedom either to endorse the dying and risen Saviour's self-identification with me ("You are what I am, and I am what you are") thus make it valid for me—or else to cancel the efficacy of his love so far as I am concerned. If I have made my decision of faith I shall for the rest of my life on earth be asked by God through every succeeding situation, whether I mean it or not. I shall have to answer again, freely, and availing myself of the wonderful resources that are now opened to me. For the same Divine Spirit that brought the Gospel message home to me by knocking at the door of my heart, is now in me as the eternally trustworthy guide of my thoughts, desires and actions.   If through faith I am one with Christ his Spirit is with my spirit—according to the invincible, triumphant logic of the love of God.   God's spiritual presence with me will make his situational call together with the Scripture message that interprets his call so strong that I am set free, in a constant struggle with my sinful nature to renew, purify and deepen my initial pledge of faith.   In the end, the Spirit of Christ will give consummate proof of his saving power.   He will demonstrate my eternal Christlikeness by raising me from death and lifting me together with all the children of God to our blessed assignments in the new Creation.

"Where the Spirit of the Lord is there is Freedom." *Again we must enlarge the concept of freedom* to denote the authority given to us by Christ and his Spirit, to exist and act in obedient, loving harmony with the all-effective will of our Creator, Redeemer and Perfector, during this time and for all eternity.

I hope I have stuck to my theme. If this has been the case the title of this paper will be self-explanatory by now. Freedom is not one of the many things man owns or carries in his mental equipment. It is a gift of God. In its New Testament understanding it represents the supernatural gift of the active nearness and ruling presence of the Spirit of Jesus Christ from whom we receive the authority to obey God in returning him the love with which he loved us first.

6. Why Is God?

Nothing is easier than to use the word God and mean nothing by it. *John Henry Newman.*

Revelation did not come in a statement, but in a person.

A filial faith is a theological faith. *Both P. T. Forsyth.*

Sed quis diligit quod ignorat? *Augustine.*

1 Corinthians 2.

WHEN I came to you, brethren, I did not come proclaiming to you the testimony of God in lofty words of wisdom. For I decided to know nothing among you except Jesus Christ and him crucified. And I was with you in weakness and in much fear and trembling; and my speech and my message were not in plausible words of wisdom, but in demonstration of the Spirit and power, that your faith might not rest in the wisdom of men but in the power of God.

Yet among the mature we do impart wisdom, although it is not the wisdom of this age or of the rulers of this age, who are doomed to pass away. But we impart a secret and hidden wisdom of God, which God decreed before the ages for our glorification. None of the rulers of this age understood this; for if they had, they would not have crucified the Lord of glory. But, as it is written,

> 'What no eye has seen, nor ear has heard,
> nor the heart of man conceived,
> What God has prepared for those who love him,'

God has revealed to us through the Spirit. For the Spirit searches everything, even the depths of God. For what person knows a man's thoughts except the spirit of the man which is in him? So also no one comprehends the thoughts of God except the Spirit of God. Now we have received not the spirit of the world, but the Spirit which is from God, that we might understand the gifts bestowed on us by God. And we impart this in words not taught by human wisdom but taught by the Spirit, interpreting spiritual truths to those who possess the Spirit.

The unspiritual man does not receive the gifts of the Spirit of God, for they are folly to him, and he is not able to understand them because they are spiritually discerned. The spiritual man judges all things, but is himself to be judged by no one. "For who has known the mind of the Lord so as to instruct him?" But we have the mind of Christ.

CONCERNING the title of this paper I shall not be apologetic. The question seems maddening, I admit. Nevertheless, I do not feel disposed to let anybody forbid me to treat my subject under this heading. This is a free country, and I am a member of a Church which was already free at a time when that involved considerable risks. Theological prohibitions are always futile. Today, when their defiance no longer entails personal danger—it is not authoritarianism against which I am up with my quest. It is, on the one hand, a feeble sentimentality, as childish as senile, that feels itself threatened by anything like thoughtful search. I remember people who stop thinking the moment they utter the word salvation, for instance. On the other hand, there is a spiritual impotence that pretends to be so greatly involved in 'action' that no room can be granted to seemingly idle questions. At the bottom of this widespread brand of theological prohibitionism looms the bad conscience of a something-must-always-be-done religion that resents concern for its foundations probably for the reason that there is very little left of them. Whether my present inquiry is idle, curious, irreverent, and whatnot depends entirely on the way it is carried out. There is, however, one *a priori* objection which I take more seriously. Its discussion can introduce my theme in a convenient manner. I shall, therefore deal with it, briefly, before I embark on my present enterprise.

Why is God? John in his first letter declares that God is love. With this declaration that is borne out by the whole Biblical Revelation my question seems to be proved futile. For is there any reason for being love? Does love need reasoning? It is strong enough to dispense with all kinds of well-intended explanations. Then, however, my question stands condemned the moment it is raised.

That was heavy artillery, yet I trust I am well entrenched. True, it is stupid to ask a person who is in love why he is in love. There are no reasons, number one, two, three and four to account for the surge of love. A husband who loves his wife because he believes that she is an excellent cook does not love her at all. Still, if a man really loves his wife so much that his love spurns all reasoning he is, nevertheless, conscious—and the more profound his love the more he is conscious—that there is nothing like mere chance in it. The myth of the winged god Cupid who shoots his arrows at random does not carry us very far. It certainly does not apply to our present subject. Remaining within the human sphere—is it altogether meaningless to speak of the sweet reasonableness of love? There is no trivial 'Why', but there is a strong inner necessity. The necessity differs from outward compulsion: True love is free and yet must be and cannot help being love. It carries its own specific rationale to which Pascal pointed with the profound claim of the logic of the heart, *la logique du coeur*. Love needs no proof: It has it. It is it. Ask a lover, and he will assure you that of all things in the world love is the last of which it could be said that it lacked true and convincing motivation. What is the rationale of love? It is not just the attraction offered by the beloved. It is rather the whole being of the beloved person, perceived as the mysterious response given to a quest. The quest itself is not some vague longing and cooing on the part of the lover. It is the hidden power that forms his personality and gives direction to his life, now being gathered up and integrated in his going out to meet the beloved and remain with him for ever.

God is not a man, and, taught by plenty of warning examples, I shall easily refrain from using artificial and deceptive analogies. At the same time, I believe that if all good things go by threes the best of all are designated with the aid of three happy anthropomorphisms. All depends on whether a metaphor is used as a metaphor and where its use leads us. I hope the objection I considered need no longer deter us from starting our inquiry.

Why is God? Can we broach our theme before we know how God is? How could we probe into the necessity of a being without a preliminary understanding of its essence? The objection is misleading. For God is not just a being; he is the source of all being. True, the two questions: 'Why is God?' and 'Who is God?' are closely interrelated—yet their interrelation bears a specific and definite character. The first question does not aim at some further progress after the second has been answered. It rather serves as a permanent check for the proper treatment of the second. For unless we are confronted with the inner necessity of the Divine being it is not God with whom we are confronted. Confrontation with God is the ultimate concern of theology. In meeting him, face to face, we are overwhelmed not by the mere fact but by the worshipful necessity of the Divine. This is, I believe, the existential truth in Anselm's famous ontological argument. It must direct our method: in asking who God is we shall submit to the tacit control of our first question until the point is reached when it steps into the foreground and reveals itself as our question.

Who is God? John testifies that God is love. Suppose that is not the only possible answer. Suppose there are a number of different answers, some of them conflicting with the one given by John. There are, of course. Nevertheless, the Johannine answer remains quite unique. The reason is that of all the various and different answers this is the only one that takes the fact and event, called Jesus Christ, into serious account. Other religions or philosophies either do not know this fact or else try to by-pass it some way or the other. I believe, however, that if Jesus Christ and the claim for which he was crucified are not taken seriously—no attempt to answer the question who God is can ultimately be taken seriously. Thus viewed, the Johannine answer has not a single competitor that could produce a real challenge to it. The love which Jesus Christ showed forth in his teaching, in his life, in his death and resurrection—that is God. The question who God is, therefore, amounts to a summons to form a concept of God that is adequate to his revelation in Jesus Christ. No human concept can be adequate to it. We are all fallible. To say this is not modesty or good manners. It is simply the constraint of an historical consciousness with which we are blessed or cursed—but I would rather say blessed—since the 18th century. So—without deceiving ourselves with vain presumptions—we shall yet have to try. And that without false modesty either. For we are entrusted with an inexhaustible treasure of Divine knowledge offered to us in Holy Scripture.

The life of Jesus Christ on earth comprehends a span of thirty-three years, perhaps less. God, however, lives from everlasting to everlasting. If the claim, concerning the Divine revelation in Jesus Christ made by several apostles and evangelists is true, then it is not just one of several aspects of the Divine being that is made known to us by Jesus Christ. It is the whole God as he always was, and will be. Nothing greater, nothing essential can be said about God apart from the last and ultimate word he has himself spoken. In speaking the word, the eschaton, Jesus Christ, God

E

has given himself to us, himself, not a part of him. He who knows Christ knows all of God.

As God has revealed himself in Christ so he is essentially, antecedently, eternally. This was clearly demonstrated in the fourth century by the great Athanasius and his successors. In our own generation it has been restated with salient lucidity and vigour by Karl Barth. About the turn of the century Peter Taylor Forsyth had made a decisive step forward in the same direction. Forsyth's approach is bolder, Barth proceeds with stricter methodical discipline. In my opinion Forsyth progresses farther than Barth though he might have gone still farther, could he have learned from the heroic discipline Barth imposed on himself, one generation later. Both theologians deserve our great respect and gratitude, and it makes me feel sorry to see some people today play off Forsyth against Barth, apparently because—to say it bluntly—the latter offers them the great disadvantage of being still alive and very much so, indeed.

In this connection another contemporary theologian with quite a different frame must be mentioned. I refer to Paul Tillich whose original and forceful reinterpretation of much in the history of Christian thought that has cruelly and falsely been tabooed as heretic is a productive incentive. Tillich has widened the theological horizon with a loving and challenging ontology, based on a profound concept of reason. His insistence on the abysmal in the Godhead and in Creation cannot be ignored without the reproach of a shallow if not frivolous lightmindedness. He who seriously differs from Tillich—and I am conscious of doing so—is due to try his strength with him, which is not an easy job though a very rewarding one.

Back to our theme. God did not, one day, make up his mind to become love, after he had been something else before. Jesus Christ reveals his entire eternal being as love. God was already love before he created the world. Or since the word 'before' in the connection seems problematical as it carries time-concepts into eternity, we better say that God is love apart from the Creation of the world. This must be said, but for the rest it is by no means necessary always to maintain that strict usage of terms.

Whom did God love when there 'was' nothing beside him to be loved? If God loves apart from Creation one might draw the conclusion that his eternal love is self-love. Now there are different kinds of self-love, and the meaning of the word is rather elastic; yet I believe that no possible interpretation of the term does justice to the New Testament revelation.

John in the prologue of his Gospel states that the beloved was with God already in the beginning. "In the beginning was the Word, and the Word was with God, and the Word was God. He was in the beginning with God." Later in the Gospel he declares that "the Father loves the Son and has given all things into his hands" (3: 35). The Word, or Son of God, became incarnate in Jesus Christ. Yet there can be no doubt that the love of his Father which Jesus Christ experienced and to which he bore witness was anything else than self-love. It was a real love between a real I and a real Thou. Yet both, the Father on the one hand and the Word made flesh on the other are God. The Word that was already with God in the beginning assumed humanity in Jesus Christ. He whom the Father loved eternally added manhood to his stature in the fulness of time. The relationship between Jesus and his Father is a genuine, personal, mutual relationship in God. When Jesus worshipped his Father and obeyed him he did not worship and obey himself. At the same time, the Divine Lordship of Jesus Christ is unambiguously attested already with Paul and with Mark. Paul, the anonymous author of the letter to the Hebrews and finally John clearly understood the mutual relationship between Jesus and his Father as the manifestation in time of an eternal relationship between two persons who equally participate in the one Divine being.

If Jesus was later called the second person in the Trinity the word second has not the meaning of a numeral. It does not denote the Son as a second in a series. This was understood by the Church Fathers. I believe that the most helpful illustration can be drawn from the grammatical concept of person. I is the first person and thou the second. When we speak of two persons in the Godhead we mean that God is both, I and Thou. We should not mean more. The classical term person originally denoted the mask an actor is wearing, then the part he is acting, the character personated in the play. We may say figuratively that the three Divine persons represent the three different parts; the same God is acting not only at the same time but all throughout eternity. Correcting the picture, we must state that God does not act the three different parts but actually lives them. For in the inexhaustible riches of the Divine being there is room for an I, a Thou and—as we shall see—a He —one God, establishing himself eternally in three reciprocal relations.

Since Augustine the West has understood the three persons as the three ways in which God is related to himself. In all three mutual relations God is love. The love of the Father to the Son I call original love, the love of the Son to the Father, return of love. God loves and is loved for all eternity. The distinction between the persons indicates that the Divine love is not what we call self-love. It is rather the contrary of it, as we shall see.

I hope we have not lost sight of our original question: Why is God? By now it has become more specific: Why is God love? Why is there love and return of love in God? According to an earlier remark our question must be used now in order to check on the authenticity of the doctrine of the Trinity, respectively its present re-interpretation so far as it has proceeded. If the question should still sound foolish, it is yet not so foolish as to expect its answer from clever or profound speculation. I can ask it only because I believe that the New Testament Revelation provides the Christian faith with the rationale of the love of God, therefore of his being.

God has revealed himself in a third way which is again inseparably connected with his incarnation in Jesus Christ. I refer to the third person in the Trinity, the Holy Spirit.

The word Christ is the translation of the Hebrew Messiah, the anointed one. In Old Testament times both king and priest were anointed with the holy oil, the king at his coronation, the priest at his installation. This was a religious ceremony with a profound meaning. In order to understand the underlying symbolism we must go back to prehistoric times when an effect of extraordinary power was ascribed to sacred ointments. Thus the anointing of a king really provided him with royal power. Christ is the Messiah, God's anointed. Yet this king was never crowned except with a crown of thorns. The Messianic ointment he received was spiritual in the most precise interpretation of the term. He was invested with the fulness of the Holy Spirit. According to Mark's Gospel the Spirit descended upon him at his baptism. According to Luke, already the slumbering consciousness of Jesus when he was still in his mother's womb was guided by the Holy Spirit since the moment that he marked the beginning of a human life without previous natural conception.

Jesus moved and lived in the power of the Spirit. That does not mean that the Spirit of God took the place of his own inner life. It rather means that the whole man Jesus yielded himself completely to the leadership of the Spirit of God. His life was a constant listening and responding. As the Spirit of God moved him, so he acted.

Jesus was a Jew, loyal to the Old Testament Law. The way, however, in which he carried out the Law was not that of a punctilious, meticulous enactment of one command after another. His obedience to the Law was a free obedience, founded on an understanding and interpretation that differed considerably from that of the contemporary Jewish leaders and brought him into sharp conflict with them. Jesus alone *knew why* he obeyed the Law. He brought the whole of it under the heading of the universal command of love for God and the neighbour. The Law, thus understood, he applied to himself in a life that was summed up by his sacrifice on the Cross.

It was the perfect submission to the guidance of the Spirit that let him understand the Old Testament as he did. The power of the Spirit whom he obeyed gives all his utterances the ring of ultimate authenticity and uncontradictory authority. Of what he said and did he was absolutely certain not in the manner of an artificially bolstered up self-confidence or stubborn cocksureness. What he said and did he won in his own hard struggles—each time a victory attained by his humble submission to the Spirit. If we understand for the spirit of a man the power that gives direction to his life, spurring, motivating and shaping it, yet never mechanically or magically but always in virtue of the man's personal decision—then we can state in all sobriety that the Spirit of God was the Spirit of Christ. So completely did Jesus subject himself to the Holy Spirit that after his resurrection all who cling to him and are one with him by faith rejoice in the same personal, spiritual guidance that ruled over his life. He who is united with Christ is led by the same Spirit that led and leads Christ. A Christian is one in whom the Spirit of Christ, the Spirit of God works. The power that makes us free to overcome ourselves and the world by deciding for God and our fellow-man is not a mere spiritual influence.

It is not something that issues from God and, once that has been the case, can be separated from him, at least in thought. It rather is and remains all personal, God himself, dwelling in the heart of his people. The inward presence of God, the Holy Spirit, provides the Christian life with an unescapable challenge to free obedience, therefore with its direction, motivation, its shape, its meaning and its certitude, in a word, with its rationale. The supreme gift of God, his Spirit, shows with his personal presence not only *what* to do, but also *why* to do it.

If God is eternally as he has revealed himself through Jesus Christ the relationship between the Spirit of God on the one hand and Jesus and his followers on the other has its antecedent correspondence in the eternal Divine life. For also of the third way of Revelation it must be said that as God has revealed himself in Christ so he is antecedently, immanently, eternally. This is not abstract reasoning. It is a necessary, personal implication of the confession of the Church that Jesus Christ is the Son of God incarnate and that those whom the Spirit leads are his brothers and sisters, children of God, "partakers of the Divine nature" (2 Pet. 1: 4). In *time*, concerning our redemption, the Spirit of God is God himself, forming with his presence the rationale of the Christian life. In *eternity*, the Spirit of God is God himself, forming the ever present rationale of the Divine life. Also here the analogy of the grammatical persons can be used. The Spirit of God is the He in God, to whom both, Father and Son, are related as they relate themselves to one another. The Holy Spirit is the foundation on which Father and Son build their mutual relationship of love. In God everything is active and personal. He has no 'back', a truth profoundly illustrated in Ezekiel's great vision. Thus all inner Divine relations are reciprocal. The fundament on which Father and Son build their mutual relationship of love is a living foundation, a founder.

Why is God love? Love is not blind. It is and remains guided by its own light. God is not love because he is love, or using a popular form of stiff, spiritless reiteration: God is not love *because* . . . The Divine love is unfathomable yet that does not prove it groundless. We can never explore its ground. Yet God has been pleased to reveal the mystery in his self-communication to us through Jesus Christ. We would never have found it ourselves, but now that we have been told, we can say with reverent conviction that it could not be otherwise but must be as we have been told. Therefore we can now argue about the ground of the love of God—that is if we do it not in a detached way of cold inference but as such that are called to draw near and in order to draw near must remove some of the obstacles they find placed in their path.

Let me start with a foolish argument. God is perfectly free to be what he pleases to be. If he is love he must have some reason for being love. For he might also be something different if he pleased. Now that is foolish, because God has revealed himself as love and to go back behind his Revelation would mean to go back behind God and so make God depend on something different from him. Admitted: it is foolish. Yet I claim that it is no longer foolish to turn the tables exactly at this point. I challenge anybody who spurns the question after the rationale of the Divine love, that it is he who does the foolish thing to go back behind God. For if there is no rationale then God is love because of a necessity that presses on him, a fate above him. If God is love 'just because' we must inevitably think of this love in terms of a big mass, trudging on through eternity. Immediately the question arises what causes that big mass to trudge on and on. If God's whole being is due to him only we must state that it is founded on and identical with an eternal act of free decision to be what he is. This decision does not belong to a dead past as eternity does not know of a dead past. Nor is God anything apart from his decision. For it covers his all. The free act of personal decision upon which God founds his whole being, is at the same time, the permanent structure of his whole being. God has lived ever since, as he is born in the eternal now. The Ancient of Days remains forever young.

The doctrine of the Trinity as I try to appropriate it describes the eternal Divine decision as one single act yet multilateral, 'multireciprocal'. God has decided for being love. The reason for his decision cannot be outside him, an impersonal 'it'. It must be in God, but not as a mere mental picture. For God does not consist of dovetailed compartments. The whole God is active in everything he does and is, or to use a classical formulation: The nature of God is simple. Therefore the motive for God's being love must be God in a third way. This third way must be again a way of love. Yet this way of love is neither original love nor returned love. It is love, forming the ground of love.

You may use psychological pictures. You may, for instance,

say that God wills himself or that God knows himself to be love. (Such illustrations require, however, a certain amount of moderation. The two I have adduced can make sense only so long as you insist that they mean absolutely the same thing. If you don't keep your hand on the bridle your horse will soon run wild. Then the Divine intellect becomes something different from the Divine will and you are attempting to establish a sort of Divine psychology, and what a primitive one to boot! Primitive or not, Divine psychology is the most impossible of all impossible disciplines. If I am not very much mistaken some trespassing on this danger zone happened from Augustine to Thomas.) God knows himself, God wills himself. However you put it, love known or love willed is never a passive object of love knowing or willing. There is no 'object' in God. Every inner Divine relationship is mutual. God known, knows God knowing. God loved, loves God loving. If you use a mirror as an illustration the picture in the mirror does not only apparently but really look back on him who looks in the mirror. The three Divine persons face one another. They are the co-eternal relations within himself that build up the being of the one only God.

Let me explain it in more personal terms as is fit in speaking of God. (I do not believe that the personal is only symbolic. I rather believe, in reference to Creation, that the impersonal is kenotic.) In deciding to be love God does not say autocratically, dictatorially: 'Let me be love'. There is nothing capricious or arbitrary about the love of God. Gerhard Teersteegen said that God is an infinitely humble being. That is not profound mystical poetry: It is good theology. Humility belongs to the very nature of the Divine love as revealed in Jesus Christ, 'gentle and lowly in heart'. That does not refer to the Son only. It refers likewise to him whom the Son has come to reveal. For Jesus Christ did not come to reveal himself. He did come to reveal the Father. In his infinite humility God does not even lord it over himself. What is at the bottom, so to speak, of the Divine decision can be symbolised under the figure of a question when the questioner does not presume to know the answer before it is actually given. It is love asking for its own ground. In the silence of eternity God the Father listens to him who, he trusts, will provide him with the answer. He entrusts himself to the guidance of God the Spirit. In perfect loyalty the Holy Spirit justifies the trust placed in him. He does not fix the Father's attention on himself. He humbly responds to the Father's quest by leading him to the Son. The Father, in complete submission to the Spirit's guidance, loves the Son. So he goes out twice: First by entrusting himself to the Spirit, second by placing his love and pouring it out according to the direction given by the Spirit. The Father does not seek himself: He seeks the Spirit. Nor does the Father mean himself: He means the Son.

I am not afraid that my statements are anthropomorphic in excess of what is legitimate. 'Service and obedience are not undivine, and not a badge of inferiority' (P. T. Forsyth, *The Person and Place of Jesus Christ*, p. 79 note). Let me therefore go on, remembering that responsibility and cowardice are mutually incompatible.

God the Son, in receiving the Father's love, returns it. The love of the Father and the love of the Son are co-eternal, yet their connection is not of a mechanical necessity. Return of love never refers to original love like the obvious solution of an arithmetic problem. It is all free and personal. If you say it stands to reason that the love of the Father is returned by the Son you are liable to state the reason to which it stands. Return of love is not an immediate reaction to original love. In between the two there is an interval, a break in eternity, comparable to that between inhaling and breathing out. In this crucial interval return of love obtains its freedom. There is no wilfulness in the Son's response to the Father's love. He does not presume to know before he actually knows. He lets the Spirit know. He humbly listens to the voice of the Spirit and thus returns the Father's love.

The same Spirit that leads the Father to the Son leads the Son back to the Father. The Son does not bask in the sunshine of the Father's love. Directed by the Spirit he goes out to meet the Father and bring his all back to him who loved him first. As the Father loves the Son so the Son loves the Father.

Jesus Christ has shown forth under the conditions of time how far love goes both ways. It means complete surrender in perfect self-denial. As Jesus was truly man there was a lag of time between the first stirring of returned love with which his life on earth began and the ultimate seal he put on it by meeting its supreme test on the Cross. His whole life on earth was the translation into human terms of his eternal life with the Father. In eternity, there is no lag between the rise of love and the ultimate self-denial that proves its reality and genuineness. Both, the love of the Son and the love of the Father it reveals, are a complete and absolute giving, a perfect abandon. The Father loses himself in loving the Son. In return the Son loses himself in the Father. So the two meet: Their self-denial has not spent itself in vain.

Also the Spirit is all self-denial. He has his whole being in keeping at the two other persons' disposal. By entrusting himself to the Spirit God the Father commissions the Spirit. The same must be said about the Son. The Holy Spirit has his all in his mission. In this interpretation the classical term of the eternal procession of the Holy Spirit from the Father and the Son can be appropriated. In leading the Father to the Son and the Son to the Father, the Spirit entirely disregards himself. God in the third way of establishing himself makes the two first converge and meet in the eternal present. The Holy Spirit has therefore of old been called 'the bond of union' in the Godhead. He rejoices not in himself but in the blessed meeting of love given and love returned. The Father and the Son rejoice in the Spirit's faithfulness and in one another. The eternal union of the three persons is the ultimate reason why there is only one God and not many. Monotheism is not self-evident. The truth it confesses has been bought by God himself at a price. The consummation of the truth is the glory and blessedness of God as declared by Christ in all four Gospel records: "He who loses his life will find it". What Christ said and did on earth has been made good in heaven before the foundation of the world. The three Divine persons are the eternal event in which God finds his life and loses it.

The truth of *God* is not and never will be the truth of a statement made about God by an observer. It is primarily the truth that lives in God and is worked out in his inner life. In order to approach it conceptually we must not attempt to understand the difference between the Father's original love and the Son's return of love.

First original love. To use an illustration. I could imagine a man (or a woman) who loves so intensely and is so entirely absorbed in his love that the idea to call his feeling love does not occur to him. He does not need the word: He has no use for it: He lives what the word means. He is not aware of himself, what he is doing, but remains totally engrossed with the beloved. In an analogous way we must conceive of the love of the Father. Prompted by the Spirit, it carries its all over to the Son.

The same may be said of the Son's return of love. The Spirit leads the Son to mean, to perceive, to know nothing but the Father who loved him first. The classical symbol of the Son's eternal generation by the Father (*Deus de Deo*) should be understood to refer exclusively to the specific character of returned love as over against original love, with the emphasis on the relations as intra-divine. The difference itself is brought out clearly by the Johannine identification of the Son with the Word. Because love is returned, because the Son loves the Father *as the loving Father* love becomes 'now' (humanly speaking for the first time) *the Divine topic*. The Father is all love. By loving him who is all love, the Son declares the Father, expresses his love with his return of it, bears witness to it, praises it, makes it manifest, characterises it. (*To characterizein* as predicated of the Son is older than Athanasius and the Council of Nicaea. Bishop Alexander used it in his second epistle. The reference is to Heb. 1: 3; *character tes hypostaseos autou*.) Therefore the Son is called the eternal Word. We do justice to John's testimony if we interpret the Word not as the one the Father speaks but as the Word that addresses itself to the Father. Original love takes no cognizance of itself. Return of love does not either, but, in being directed towards original love, speaks and reveals it. The Son is the Revealer in God, the witness (antecedent to his work on earth which he summed up before Pilate as a witness: Jn. 18: 37) and the work he accomplishes is the *eternal truth* (*ibid.*). *For the truth about love can only be expressed with its actual return.* And since the return of love is a holy and passionate Divine acknowledgment of first love it can never be separated from what we call in human translation *worship and adoration*. The Inspirator of the work of truth is called the Spirit of truth. Led by the Spirit, the Son glorifies the Father. In God's eternal life truth, glory and blessedness are all one.

I cannot now point to the theological and philosophical implications of the concept of truth I have outlined. They must, of course, be worked out fresh without attempting sterile deductions from what can never be considered a kind of 'axiom'. Time does not, however, fail me to pay grateful and enthusiastic tribute to the vessel of Grace, Søren Kierkegaard, whose existential discovery of existential truth tore the whole concept out of the literally yawning abyss of theological and philosophical oblivion.

I have tried to make a contribution toward executing the theological programme which P. T. Forsyth called 'the moralising of dogma'. The method observed is, in the words of the same thinker, that of a 'metaphysic of the conscience'. In the last analysis it is dictated by the fact that theology has but one starting-point: Jesus Christ. If it leads anywhere, it leads back to him. In this blessed circuit theology has its whole task and meaning. Mindful of that, I shall close in drawing some simple personal inferences. I shall make three points, very briefly, yet must confess that apart from these consequences nothing I said was worth saying.

First: What does God demand of us people? Trust, obedience, love. Well, what God demands of us he is practising himself from everlasting to everlasting. God, the Father, God, the Son, entrust themselves to the leading presence of the Spirit and submit to him in loving each other. The Spirit, for his part, is the faithful and obedient executor of his mission. So God does not impose on us anything he did not eternally impose on himself.

Second: On our own behalf and on behalf of others we complain daily about pain, suffering, privation, frustration. In the Holy Trinity we have a picture of God, giving himself up entirely. None of the three Persons withholds from the other anything he has or is. God is unspeakably rich because he is unspeakably poor. 'There was a Calvary above which is the mother of us all' (P. T. Forsyth). As some mystics put it: God is and is not. He finds his whole being in rising triumphantly out of the nothingness of infinite self-denial. The nothing itself, the true, original, antecedent nothing derives from the love of God. It is in God in all eternity. So we should not fancy that God lives a good life in heaven while we poor folks down below must fret ourselves and be plagued every day. God lives a good life, indeed, a life of perfect blessedness—but even the best Christian, so long as death has not delivered him from his innate selfishness, would not dare to wish living this kind of life for a single moment, if he knew what it was like.

And yet we are called to participate in the Divine life of glorious, everlasting love. For we are made the children of God, his next of kin through Jesus Christ, who at the centre of human history repeated the eternal sacrifice he makes at the bosom of the Father. Irenaeus wrote: 'In his infinite love God was made what we are that he might make us what he is'. Christ died for our sins. In his death and resurrection he made himself one with us in order that we, by enshrining him in our hearts, may die with our sins and rise without them ratifying with our faith the union he has established. This is my third point and it gathers up the first and the second. Those who are one with Christ receive the Spirit. The Spirit challenges and empowers us to practise trust, obedience and love in the school of self-denial, called time. Through this school we must pass in order to, ultimately, enjoy the fellowship of eternal love, to participate actively in the event of truth by glorifying the Father in accompanying the Son on his everlasting return to him. For this we are made.

7. Fundamental Differences Between Judaism and Christianity

IT HAS OFTEN BEEN SAID that Jews and Christians pray to the same God. That is true only if they really pray, otherwise it qualifies as a glib phrase, often an excuse for dodging the question of truth. But if they pray the same God will answer.

That does not, however, make every Christian prayer fit for inclusion in a Jewish prayer book or vice versa. From their prayers offered to the same God, but set against our different theological backgrounds, the fundamental differences between the two faiths can be brought into focus, sharper perhaps than by any other form of comparison. The fact that we pray to the same God does unite us, yet we are divided by our fundamental disagreements.

For this reason the present study will be geared to a prayer that is both profoundly Jewish and profoundly Christian. It attests in the simplest and most concise form the Jewish-Christian faith in God. The prayer which Jesus taught his disciples forms the pattern of Christian worship, private and public. Yet everything in it bears a definite Jewish stamp. It is thoroughly indebted not only to the Old Testament but also to Rabbinic thought and piety. The numerous parallels are not limited to words and phrases. Even where verbal similarities are not strongly attested, as in the case of the first clause of the third petition ("Thy will be done"), the agreement in point of content is evident.

It has been stated by Jewish writers that any faithful Jew could offer this prayer. This is true, but if he did, the meaning would be radically different. To show this is the purpose of this brief study.

While bearing the whole of the Lord's Prayer in mind, I will limit myself to the first petition: "Our Father who art in heaven, hallowed be thy name" (Mt. 6: 9). Luke in his Gospel offers a shorter form: "Father, hallowed be thy name" (11: 2). E. F. Scott[1] maintains the originality of Matthew's version, while Ernst Lohmeyer[2] has made it probable that the differences are due to early liturgical use in different parts of Palestine.

The Matthean form is the one used (with some variations) in public worship, and through the influence of public worship in private Christian prayer.

This fact must determine my choice as I will treat of the petition in its churchly interpretation. It is probable that the disciples of Jesus used his prayer in their common worship from the time it had been given them. It is beyond doubt for the Christian faith that the radical and definite understanding of the teaching of Jesus including his prayer was received by the Church after the Resurrection. It is only in the light of the Church's understanding of the Lord's Prayer that the fundamental differences between Christianity and Judaism can be brought out.

1

IN the Old Testament the understanding of God or Israel's Father occurs in different layers of tradition.

In Exodus 4: 22 f., Moses in the name of the Lord says to Pharaoh "Israel is my first-born son". This becomes the basis for a command. Israel is the Lord's precious creation so Pharaoh must let him go lest the Lord slay Pharaoh's first-born son.

This statement of God's paternal relation to Israel is exceptional. It addresses neither the Lord nor Israel. This makes it particularly valuable for our present purpose: Even in those words spoken to a stranger *the meaning* of the Father-son relationship is revealed by the context:

"Thus says the Lord, Israel is my first-born son, and I say to you, Let my son go that he may serve me," or, "worship me" as rendered by the new Jewish translation.[3]

The passage reveals two essential features concerning the fatherhood of God. First, the birth of Israel as a nation is due to Divine action in history, the Exodus event. Father means Creator but not in the sense of the whole world's Creator, still less of physical propagation of which no traces are found in the Old Testament. God has elected Israel and made it his people by bringing them out of the land of Egypt, the house of bondage. On this act of creative election rests Israel's faith in its mighty, merciful sovereign Lord.

Second, it is clearly stated what the Lord's election love implies for the people: "that they may worship me". The fact that the

Lord created Israel with an act of salvation in history means to
the people infinitely more than what any theoretical statement by a
historian could assert: It calls for Israel's response. This response
is not due to an external, legal obligation but follows from the
nature of the case. Because the Lord is Israel's Father the people
must express their filial position with their actions, in this case,
national worship. Pharaoh must let the people go that they put
into practice their vocation as the Lord's first-born son.

In other pertinent texts the people's active response to their
Father who had made them consists of *filial obedience, faithfulness,
loyalty* for the lack of which they are reproved in

Deuteronomy 32: 6: "Do you thus requite the Lord,
                   you foolish and senseless people?
                   Is he not your father, who created you,
                   who made you and established you?"

Hosea 11: 1: "When Israel was a child, I loved him,
             and out of Egypt I called my son.
             The more I called them,
             the more they went from me."

Isaiah 1: 2: "Sons have I reared and brought up,
             but they have rebelled against me."

Jeremiah 3: 19: "And I thought you would call me, My Father,
                and would not turn from following me."

Filial reverence

in accepting God's authoritative decision:

Isaiah 45: 10 f.: "Woe to him who says to a father,
                  'What are you begetting?'
                  or to a woman,
                  'With what are you in travail?'
                  Thus says the Lord
                  The Holy One of Israel, and his Maker:
                  Will you question me about my children
                  or command me concerning the work of
                  my hands?"

in worship:

Malachi 1: 6: "If then I am a father, where is my honour?"

Trust in the Father who consoles and rescues them in their affliction as in

Jeremiah 31: 9: "With weeping they shall come,
                 and with consolations I will lead them
                 back,
               I will make them walk by brooks of water,
                 in a straight path in which they shall not
                 stumble;
               for I am a father to Israel,
                 and Ephraim is my first-born."

Trust in the Father's redemptive compassion

Isaiah 63: 16: "For thou art our Father,
                 though Abraham does not know us
                 and Israel does not acknowledge us:
               Thou, O Lord, art our Father,
                 our Redeemer from old is thy name."

                                    (Cp. Is. 64: 8; 63: 8 f.)

Psalm 103: 13: "As a father pities his children,
                 so the Lord pities those who fear him."

In Malachi 2: 10, the condemnation of marriages with the heathen
and of divorces is derived from Israel's filial position.

"Have we not all one father? Has not one God created us?
Why then are we faithless to one another, profaning the covenant
of our fathers?"

Those who have the Lord for their Father are members of one
family, therefore by the very nature of the relation they are bound
to mutual faithfulness.

Finally, a quite specific prohibition in Deuteronomy calls for our
special attention in the context of this study:

"You are the sons of the Lord your God; you shall not cut yourselves or make any baldness on your foreheads for the dead. For
you are a people holy to the Lord your God, and the Lord has
chosen you to be a people for his own possession, out of all the
peoples that are on the face of the earth" (Dt. 14: 1).

The Israelites must strictly avoid pagan rites of mourning for the
dead because they are the sons of the Lord their God. They must
loathe what he loathes. *Like father like children.* Again this is
not the imposition of an external statute. The imitation of God

F

follows from Israel's holiness which, as the context clearly shows, consists in their belonging to their Father as his exclusive, precious possession.

2

THE concept of God's fatherly possession of, and rule over, Israel is closely related to that of Divine kingship (see for instance Ex. 15: 18; 19: 6; Num. 23: 21; Dt. 33: 5; Jdg. 8: 23; 1 Sam. 8: 7; 12: 12).   Both terms are metaphors, the one taken from the family relationships, the other from political covenant language.   Both frequently occur together in the Jewish Prayer Book.   The juxtaposition is ancient, as for instance in the litany recited on the Ten Penitential Days preceding the Day of Atonement where every petition begins with the praise: 'Our Father, our King'.

Which term is older is a moot question.   It seems probable that both combined go back to the Mosaic period.   Their common root lies in Israel's faith in being *owned* by her Maker and Saviour God. The great covenant promise that precedes the promulgation of the Ten Commandments is introduced by a strong and tender reminder of the Lord's parental mercy:

"You have seen what I did to the Egyptians, and how I bore you on *eagle's wings* and brought you to myself" (Ex. 19: 4).

Then follows the covenant promise:

"Now therefore, if you will obey my voice and keep my covenant" (which at this juncture they were still free to accept or to reject, Cp. v. 8), "you shall be my own possession among all peoples; for all the earth is mine, and you shall be to me a kingdom of priests and a holy nation" (*ibid*. 5 f.).

Here is the origin of the profound joy that characterises Israel's faith and worship.   There is no greater delight than to be the treasured possession of the Lord of all the earth.   The joy of being owned by their Lord shall determine Israel's mind and actions. The Lord owns them as their loving Father to whom the whole nation and every one of its members can and must entrust themselves wholeheartedly in every life situation.   He owns them as their almighty King who leads and rules his people with perfect justice and wisdom.   Their due obedience to him derives from both his kingship and fatherhood yet is in a more personal and heartfelt manner implied in the Father-son relationship.   Filial trust, reverence, love, submission.   All those different terms are but various expressions for one and the same response to him to whom the people from the beginning of its history and to its end owes itself entirely.

3

IN rabbinic Judaism the invocation of God as Israel's Father ("Our Father") occurs very often. George Foot Moore claims as a characteristic feature of the piety of the first two centuries A.D. 'the increasing frequency with which God is addressed as "Father" or "Father in heaven" '.[4]   Jesus took the address 'Our Father' not from the Old Testament where it does not occur in the address to God but rather from living Jewish tradition.[5]   Prayer obliges him who offers it.   From the Father-son relationship the faithful Jew drew an 'all-sufficient reason and motive for abstaining from what he forbids'.[6]   Though the obedience thus motivated is not limited to laws of prohibition.

As in the Old Testament so with the contemporaries of Jesus and the succeeding generations: the Father is the only refuge of his people in whom they place their confidence and whose mercy they implore in times of need and affliction.   As in the Old Testament, the Father-son relationship calls from its nature for the blending of trust and obedience in the life response of the people.

This must be taken into account in order to understand the intimate connection between the fatherhood of God and the hallowing of his name.   Those who call on God as their Father will pray 'like this'.

"Hallowed be thy name."

In every petition God is asked to act.   But that is not identical with telling him what he ought to do.   Therefore, though the Father is the logical subject of the sentence ('Hallow thy name') the Greek uses the passive aorist.   The Aramaic original probably had the reflexive *hitpa'al* as in the Kaddish and other rabbinical prayers: May thy name hallow itself.   The usage is one of humble reverence.

The hallowing of the Name (*kiddush hashem*) is equally a central Jewish and a central Christian concern.   The Kaddish prayer, a series of doxologies offered in the daily worship of the Synagogue, starts with the words: 'Magnified and sanctified be his great name . . .'.   There are many other parallels.

The doxological characters of the Kaddish as well as the first

petition in the Lord's Prayer does not make either less of a genuine
petition.   In many Psalms God is praised with a call to the worshipping congregation, to the Psalmist's own soul, to all that breathes,
to praise the name of the Lord.   In the prayer under consideration
God is praised with the petition that he may cause his name to be
praised.

This prayer has grown from Old Testament soil.   We read in
Ezekiel: "Thus says the Lord God: It is not for your sake, O house
of Israel, that I am about to act, but for the sake of my holy name,
which you have profaned among the nations to which you came.
And I will vindicate the holiness of my great name, which has been
profaned among the nations, and which you have profaned among
them, and the nations will know that I am the Lord, says the Lord
God, when through you I vindicate my holiness before their eyes"
(Ezek. 36: 22 f.).

The name of God is God himself.   His holy name is the Lord
in his holiness.   God promises to vindicate (literally, to hallow,
to sanctify) himself by actions of judgment and grace.   By what
he is doing with Israel he will teach the nations to know, that is,
to acknowledge him.

With his promised eschatological action the Lord will hallow
his name for the benefit of the nations.   According to normative
Judaism Israel alone is commanded and privileged to sanctify his
name with its own present life of devotion and dedication.[7]   Therefore, it asks its Father for the inner strength to accomplish the
Kiddush Hashem.   George Foot Moore states that in the age of
the Tannaim (first two centuries A.D.) the hallowing of the name 'is
developed into what may fairly be regarded as the most characteristic features of Jewish ethics both as principle and as a motive'.[8]

The petition has since of old presented a challenge to thought:
If God is holy, what can man add to his holiness?   The problem
occupied the mind of Rabbis[9] and Church Fathers.[10]

The Jewish answer is: The name of God is hallowed (synonyms:
glorified, magnified.   Cp. the Kaddish prayer and Jn. 12: 28, Lk. 1:
46) by loving devotion to him, by being active in the observation
of the law, to the point of laying down one's life for the sake of the
Name.[11]   Martyrdom is the supreme form of glorifying God.

The rational connection between the hallowing of the name and
the keeping of the law has been a matter of reflection in Judaism
at least since Philo.   Tannaitic Midrashim referred in this connec-

tion to places like Leviticus 19: 2: "You shall be holy; for I the Lord your God am holy", or Leviticus 11: 44: "For I am the Lord your God; hallow yourselves, therefore, and be holy, for I am holy".

God is hallowed by imitation of his purity and mercy. R. Hama ben Hanina (second half, second century A.D.) said, 'As he clothes the naked (Gen. 3: 21), so do thou clothe the naked. He visits the sick (Gen. 18: 1); do thou also visit the sick. He comforts mourners (Gen. 25: 11); do thou also comfort mourners. He buries the dead (Dt. 34: 6); do thou also bury the dead'.[12]

God has sanctified Israel in separating them from the nations by giving them his law in order that they in turn might sanctify him by keeping his law. The thought is expressed in the K'dushah offered at the evening service: 'Praised are you, O Lord our God, King of the Universe, who sanctified us through his commandments . . .'.

Because the Lord is Israel's Owner they are due to affirm his ownership with their words of worship and lives of obedience. Thus they will spiritually return themselves to their holy Founder, Saviour, Sovereign. In their surrender of trust, response of worship, purity of life and brotherliness of mutual relations the name of God shall be reflected as in a mirror. The hallowing of the name is the living expression of the divine-human relationship, 'truth in action' (Martin Buber). Kierkegaard described 'existential truth' as a two-way movement. In this sense God's love for his people appears for a second time in their love for him and for one another. This is the ultimate meaning of the imitation of God by his people. Let it be suggested in passing that even those Old Testament and subsequent Jewish ideas that seem so remote from pure faith as is the expectation of Israel's eschatological rule over the nations, should be set against the theological background sketched above. Their origin is not fierce nationalistic passion or selfish ambition but rather an anticipation of the authority with which the people of God hope to be invested in the coming age, God's seal on their imitation of him.

4

THE Christian understanding of the fatherhood of God and the hallowing of his name is characterised *formally*, by a far higher and more radical evaluation of Israel's prophets than prevails in Judaism. For normative Judaism the teaching of the prophets provides an authoritative, divinely given commentary on the Torah, and this view has had its effect on all branches of Judaism despite the great variety of convictions and views held.

For the Church the Torah cannot be understood apart from the prophets. It is only through prophetic revelation that the testimony of the Law and the other writings can be opened up as a testimony to the redemption of the world by Jesus Christ.

This is not to conjure up the ghosts of the Messianic proof-texts of old. More often than not in the history of Christian-Jewish polemic the Jewish rejection of quotations torn out from their context was correct. The arguing from isolated sentences has been refuted by two hundred years of painstaking critical research and historical background study. Theologically, it tended to intellectualise and thus neutralise much of the living message of the prophets. According to a famous anecdote Hillel the Elder (c. 60 B.C.-A.D. 20) said to a proselyte who wanted to learn the whole Torah while standing on one leg, 'What is hateful to thee do not do to thy fellowmen'.

If I were to sum up the revelation by the prophets from Amos to Malachi while standing on one leg I would reply: 'Israel's holy and merciful Lord will say "yes" to his people only after he has said "no" to them'.

For the prophets made it crystal clear that the people which God has called out of the nations to hallow his name did not and would not hallow his name. This is not a reparable breach of obedience. It stems from the root of Israel's historical existence. It goes back to the foundation of the people. For this is the way Hosea sees it as documented by a text which I will now quote again:

"When Israel was a child, I loved him,
    and out of Egypt I called my son."

But then the prophet adds:

"The more I called them,
    the more they went from me" (Hos. 11: 1 f.).

In this they persisted in the following centuries when God prospered them and delivered them from their foes:

"Israel is a luxuriant vine
  that yields its fruit.
The more his fruit increased
  the more altars he built . . .
Their heart is false;
  now they must bear their guilt.
The Lord will break down their altars,
  and destroy their pillars" (*ibid.* 10: 1 f.).

It is of crucial importance to realise that for the prophets Israel's sin is not only what we call actual sinning.   It is *original sin.*

So in Jeremiah: "From the day that your fathers came out of the land of Egypt to this day, I have persistently sent all my servants the prophets to them, day after day, yet they did not listen to me, or incline their ear, but stiffened their neck" (Jer. 7: 25 f.).

"Can the Ethiopian change his skin
  or the leopard his spots?
Then also you can do good
  who are accustomed to do evil" (*ibid.* 13: 23).

Ezekiel is no less radical: "On this day when I chose Israel, I swore to the seed of the house of Jacob, making myself known to them in the land of Egypt, I swore to them, saying, I am the Lord your God.   On that day I swore to them that I would bring them out of the land of Egypt into a land that I had searched out for them, a land flowing with milk and honey, the most glorious of all lands.   And I said to them, Cast away the detestable things your eyes feast on, every one of you, and do not defile yourselves with the idols of Egypt; I am the Lord your God.   But they rebelled against me and would not listen to me; they did not every man cast away the detestable things their eyes feasted on, nor did they forsake the idols of Egypt" (Ezek. 20: 5-10).

The history of the chosen people starts with their apostasy. Ezekiel's 'historical excursions aim at showing that it is neither single trespasses nor the failure of one generation, but a deep-seated inability to render obedience, even a resistance against God that revealed itself already on the first day when Israel began to exist'.[13]

But did not the prophets call Israel to return to God, to repent?

Cannot the Jewish doctrine of the unlimited efficiency of repentance[14] claim the full support of famous biblical texts as, e.g.:

"Though your sins are like scarlet,
  they shall be as white as snow;
though they are red like crimson,
  they shall become like wool" (Is. 1: 18)?

No doubt they would have, but did the people heed the prophet's call to repentance? "But you refuse and rebel," the prophet adds to his conditional promise (*ibid*. 20). A prophet is not primarily an admonisher: he is a revealer. The people had to be called to repent so that their impenitence, the hold of sin over them, might be brought to light. The summons to repentance from which I quoted must be seen in the light of Isaiah's call to the prophetic ministry:

"Go and say to this people:

'Hear and hear, but do not understand:
  see and see, but do not perceive'.
Make the heart of this people fat,
  and their ears heavy
and shut their eyes,
  lest they see with their eyes,
and hear with their ears,
  and understand with their hearts,
and turn and be healed" (Is. 6: 9 f. Cp. Mk. 4: 11 f.).

Such utterances, not confined to Isaiah, cannot be attenuated or explained away. The prophecy of hardening translated into conceptual terms is to the effect *that not only what the prophet proclaims but likewise the fact that his proclamation is rejected forms an integral part of the Divine revelation through the prophet.* Through the marvellous work the Lord is going to do "the wisdom of their wise men shall perish, and the discernment of their discerning men shall be hid" (*ibid*. 29: 14. See 1 Cor: 19).

Repentance is beyond human capacity. The synagogue prays every day in the Tefillah (Amidah):

'Our Father, bring us back to Your Torah;
Our King, draw us near to Your service;
Lead us back, truly repentant before You.
Praised are You, O Lord, who welcomes repentance.'

The Church can share this prayer if it applies the eschatological proclamation of Mark 1: 15: "The time is fulfilled, and the kingdom of God is at hand; repent, and believe in the gospel". We must reject the good Jewish but miserable Christian assertion of the 'fulfillability of the law' (H. J. Schoeps). The above quotations from the prophets definitely point in the direction of Paul's confessions and teaching in Romans ch. 7. For the confession of his failure to obey the law despite his passionate endeavours must not be reduced to psychological half-truths. It draws the consequence from the prophetic revelation of original sin. The doctrine of original sin by no means exclusively depends on the profound, heart touching sermon by the so-called Jahwist in Genesis 3.

Neither repentance nor the prayer for true repentance are at man's disposal. In Isaiah's and his disciples' prophecies repentance is the subject of a promise given to the remnant that is to be left after the Lord has accomplished his astonishing work of destruction: Isaiah 7: 3 (she'ar yashuv: a remnant shall return; 4: 3; 10: 20; 11: 16; 28: 5).

Thus the hallowing of the Name is relegated from the past and present to a promised future: "Behold, the days are coming, says the Lord, when I will make a new covenant with the house of Israel and the house of Judah, not like the covenant which I made with their fathers when I took them by the hand to bring them out of the land of Egypt, my covenant which they broke, though I was their husband, says the Lord. But this is the covenant which I will make with the house of Israel after those days, says the Lord: I will put my law within them, and I will write it upon their hearts; and I will be their God, and they shall be my people" (Jer. 31: 31 ff.).

This covenant will be founded on the forgiveness of Israel's sin (ibid. 34). It is not new in the sense that the old will be abolished: What will be abolished is Israel's sin. The covenant "which they broke" will be renewed in its divinely intended purity and force. That is proved by the resumption of the ancient priestly covenant promise: "I will be their God, and they shall be my people" (Cp., for instance, Gen. 17: 8; Ex. 29: 45; Lev. 26: 12; Dt. 29: 13).

What does then the newness of the covenant mean? That the Exodus event will no longer represent the constitutive factor for the faith and historical memory of the redeemed Israel. (See Jer. 23: 7.) The revelation of God in response to which they will know and serve him is the forgiveness of their sin and the gift of a new heart. "I will give them one heart and one way, that they may fear me for ever" (*ibid.* 32: 39).   To fear God means to obey his will (L. Koehler).

Ezekiel adds to what is substantially the same promise an explicit reference to the new spirit: "A new heart I will give you, and a new spirit I will put within you, and I will take out of your flesh the heart of stone and give you a heart of flesh" (Ezek. 36: 26).   Spirit denotes 'the motive power of the soul', 'the energy, as we would say, which is raised and leads the soul to certain acts'.[15]

Instead of a new covenant Ezekiel speaks of a "covenant of peace" (34: 25; 37: 26), blissful harmony between a holy, merciful God and his obedient people.

The most radical formulation for the new foundation of Israel's promised salvation is presented by the great prophet of the Babylonian exile, the second Isaiah.   He declares that the exodus shall no more be remembered.   Though it is not at all forgotten by the prophet.   He understands it as the primitive church would do later, typologically.

As the Lord once brought Israel out of Egypt so will he deliver the exiles from their Babylonian captivity, but this deliverance will throw the first Exodus into the shade:

"Thus says the Lord,
  who makes a way in the sea,
a path in the mighty waters,
  who brings forth chariot and horse,
army and warrior;
  they lie down, they cannot rise,
  they are extinguished, quenched like a wick" (Is. 43: 16 f.).

This is clearly a reference to the crossing of the Red Sea and overthrow of the Egyptian army.   But then the prophet continues:

"Remember not the former things,
  nor consider the things of old.
Behold, I am doing a new thing;
  now it springs forth, do you not perceive it?
I will make a way in the wilderness
  and rivers in the desert" (*ibid.* 18 f.).

The old things not to be remembered and considered are the Exodus, and in a wider sense intended by the prophet 'the sacred history from the call of Abraham till the destruction of Jerusalem.'[16] 'With this reference to the new Exodus Deutero-Isaiah touches Israel's fundamental, original confession (*das Urbekenntnis Israels*); he even musters all possibilities of persuasion to draw away his contemporaries from that event on which their faith has rested hitherto and to direct their faith towards the new and greater event.'[17]

Yet this new and greater event is described typologically, in terms of the first Exodus (see e.g. Is. 42: 13; 48: 21; 52: 12). God's saving action will fulfill on a far larger scale and in the most astounding manner what Israel's ancient, sacred traditions had already attested concerning his character, power and attitude to his people. Yet the Lord's future deeds remain inscrutable and incalculable. For he will forever refuse to put himself at the disposal of a backsliding people—and here the greatest prophet of comfort proclaims Israel's original sin no less sternly than his predecessors:

"They [the new things promised] are created now, not long ago;
   before today you have never heard of them,
lest you should say, 'Behold, I knew them'.
You have never heard, you have never known,
from of old your ear has not been opened.
For I knew that you would deal very treacherously,
and that from birth you were called a rebel" (*ibid.* 48: 7 f.).

The promised salvation in no sense whatever presupposes Israel's obedience. The Christian term 'prevenient grace' can be applied without hesitation. Repentance does not precede but follows salvation. Deutero-Isaiah's proclamation of world-wide repentance must be seen in this perspective. As Israel will be redeemed from sin and punishment so will the nations be. Israel will be made a witness (43: 10; 44: 8; 55: 4), a divinely given sign to the world of nations. For Israel is the representative people, the people of revelation. Through what God is going to do with them the nations will be convicted of their original sinfulness. They will "in shame" (41: 11; 42: 17; 45: 24) throw away their idols as they turn to Israel's and their own Saviour.

Till then, Israel and the nations are under God's judgment. How far do the Divine judgments extend? According to the prophets, to the end. Through destruction to a new creation; through the end to a new beginning; through doom to acceptance; through death to life—that is the meaning of Israel's, therefore of all history, as revealed by God's interpretive messengers. The human answer it calls forth is quite different from the protestations of man's ability to keep the law and if one breaks it to return through the ever open gate of *teshuvah* (repentance).

The Old Testament has nothing of this. The doctrine of the so-called freedom of a so-called will with which man lords it over himself and which he owns as I own my pen-knife and keep it handy in my pocket is foreign to, and flies in the face of, biblical revelation. Man's abysmal rebellion against God cannot be remedied by himself or by the merits of the fathers of which the Old Testament betrays no knowledge despite the rendering of Genesis 15: 6 in the new Jewish translation of the Torah: "And because he (Abraham) put his trust in the Lord, he reckoned it to his merit".

The true response made by Israel's faithful remnant to the divine indictments and promises can be epitomised in the words of the 130th Psalm:

"Out of the depths I cry to thee, O Lord!
　　Lord hear my voice!
Let thy ears be attentive
　　to the voice of my supplications!
If thou, O Lord, shouldst mark iniquities,
　　Lord, who can stand?
But there is forgiveness with thee,
　　that thou mayest be feared.
I wait for the Lord, my soul waits,
　　and in his word I hope;
my soul waits for the Lord
　　more than watchmen for the morning,
more than watchmen for the morning.
O Israel, hope in the Lord!
　　for with the Lord there is steadfast love,
　　and with him is plenteous redemption.
And he will redeem Israel
　　from all his iniquities."

5

THE Christian faith holds that this cry out of the depths that truly expresses the human predicament has been definitely and ultimately answered in Jesus Christ. It is he for whom the faithful in Israel had been waiting and hoping. They did not know him, but their waiting and hoping faith leaped across the centuries ahead. They touched the fringe of the coming Saviour's robe and were healed.

That holds also of all those who through ignorance of Christ or from distorted pictures, old or modern, that had sunk into their minds since childhood, are prevented from responding to the challenge of the One who is both the Revealer and the content of revelation. Divine revelation can only be received in actual response to it. By a responsible decision of faith a man realises that God in Christ has communicated himself to us sinners, forgiven us, and freed us from our sin, to grant us the power to withstand its assaults and along with it the present anticipation of faith must be worked, constantly, into the whole length and breadth, width and depth of everyday life. Thus the intent of the Old Testament Law is to be fulfilled by those who are by faith united to its Fulfiller and incorporated in his Body, the Church.

This is not perfection yet. Far from it. It is the resurgence out of the depth of the new man whose daily oppression by the old man constrains him to learn that there is no salvation apart from Christ. Yet in this painful struggle the hallowing of the name is imputed to those who daily pray for it to the Father who with his Son sent his second self straight into their hearts.

For Jesus did not only come to preach the good news of the fulfilment of time and the dawning of God's new order. He is himself the good news.

He called God "my Father" in an incomparable sense (Mt. 15: 13; 16: 17; 26: 29). To the Church the Father is primarily the Father of Jesus. Because he is the Father of the Son he is also the Father of all those who believe in the Son.

When Peter at Caesarea Philippi made his confession to Jesus as "the Christ, the Son of the living God" (Mt. 16: 16) Jesus answered: "Blessed are you, Simon Bar-Jona! For flesh and blood has not revealed this to you, but my Father who is in heaven". Nothing would seem more natural than to call God who had at this juncture revealed the Son to Peter 'your', Peter's Father. 'If nevertheless Jesus says, "my Father" the legitimate conclusion is that the knowledge of the Son means also the knowledge of the Father. As he is "my Father", thus, and therefore he is also "your Father".'[18] 'Because he has sent the eschatological

Perfector invested with eschatological might, word, and deed, therefore God has become the Father who has mercy upon the poor and
therefore demands the most of them: "You therefore must be perfect, as your heavenly Father is perfect" (Mt. 5: 48).' [19]   When Jesus
praises the Father, Lord of heaven and earth, for having revealed
these things to babes (Mt. 11: 25) he sees God's eschatological
fatherhood revealed in the election of the babes (or "the simple",
New English Bible).   'Because he is his Father, he can allow himself to be called their Father by the simple; they therefore dare
pray: "Our Father who art in heaven".'   For 'God is Father
because he is now beginning to perfect what he created and to
fulfil what he promised'.[20]

'The revelation which Jesus proclaims and himself is' [21] cannot
be placed on a level with the prior historical revelations as they are
recorded in the Old Testament, "The old has passed away, behold,
the new has come" (2 Cor. 5: 17). 'The fatherhood of God that
reveals itself in the actions of Jesus has "become new"; it draws its
power already from the coming age whose proclaimer and effecter
the Son of man is . . . One will now realise that the primitive church
saw in the cry, "Abba! Father!", the clearest and purest expression
of its new faith'.[22]   Lohmeyer's far-reaching form-critical investi-
gations result in the understanding of the Father name as the common root of the Synoptic and Johannine traditions,[23] the nucleus
of the original teaching of Jesus.

If the Son is the fountain of salvation the possessive pronoun
'our' in 'our Father' receives a new sense.   The Church with its
faith lives already in the coming age.   'All historical ties have
ceased, blood and soil, the glory and the mourning, the splendour
and the misery of history; what remains as the only bond that
unites those who pray is "our Father in heaven", the dialogue with
him out of inward care, need, guilt but also from the knowledge of
eschatological grace obtained.'[24]

The praying community is formed by the Father and consists
of those who affirm the Father's grace with the prayer that Jesus
gave them.   The title for addressing God as Father is no longer
membership in the Jewish people, either by birth or by adoption.
All those can say, 'Father' who were given power to become God's
children as they believe in the name of the Son (Jn. 1: 12).   And
those who are the Father's are one another's.

That leads us to the Christian understanding of the predication 'in heaven'. With the Rabbis the expression is employed to distinguish God from earthly fathers.[25] The Christian interpretation implies the vision of the new Jacob's ladder, "heaven opened, and the angels of God ascending and descending upon the Son of man" (John 1: 51). The Church's prayerful acknowledgement of salvation is no longer geared to Mt. Sinai or Mt. Zion. In the Epistle to the Hebrews Jerusalem is interpreted typologically as the heavenly city and contrasted with Mt. Sinai (Heb. 12: 18-24). In John's Gospel the attachment of the name of God to an earthly sanctuary is replaced by his ubiquitous personal presence realised in worshipful recognition: "The hour is coming when neither on this mountain nor in Jerusalem will you worship the Father. The hour is coming and now is, when the true worshippers will worship the Father in spirit and truth, for such the Father seeks to worship him. God is spirit, and those who worship him must worship in spirit and truth" (Jn. 4: 21-24). The twofold employment of the Father name in this passage is characteristic of the new interpretation it received by Jesus.

Jesus not only taught us to pray the Father for the hallowing of his name by ourselves and by all (for we offer this prayer not only on our own behalf but also vicariously for all mankind; it is intercessory as well as petitionary); he also guarantees its answering. This can be shown with the aid of conceptual material used earlier in this study.

Jesus said to Thomas: "I am the way, and the truth, and the life; no one comes to the Father, but by me" (Jn. 14: 6); and to Pontius Pilate: "For this I was born, and for this I have come into the world, to bear witness to the truth" (*ibid.* 18: 37). God is love. With his response of love to his Father Jesus reflected and thus bore effective witness to the Father's love. God's love appeared for a second time in the word and work of the Son. Love for God in the Bible is not primarily a matter of emotion. It is obedience, rendered with heart, mouth and hand. In loving the Father the Son carried out the work he had given him to do. He fulfilled his mission of self-identification with the sinners whom he came to seek and save. Those who with their faith accept the Saviour as he unites himself to them receive their share in his 'doubling' of the Father's love. They are made Christ's witnesses. (Cp. Is. 43: 10, 12; 44: 8; Lk. 24: 48; Acts 1: 8.) In witnessing to him, they witness to the Father, and thus imitate God. Under the new covenant the hallowing of the name consists in a Christlike mind and life.

This new life presupposes the sinner's death. The message of the prophets that destruction must precede salvation is not a sublime poetic generality. The Gospel of Christ brings every one who has ears to hear to the conviction that having deserted and betrayed God, he must empty the cup of God's No to the dregs. God saves me by judging me. What I have desired all the time, though I never ceased to cover my desire with false and futile excuses, was just to be left alone by God and by my fellow men. What I wanted I must get, for in no other way can the lethal thrust of my existence be reversed. Being forsaken by God, having lost God, my fellow men, myself—only thus can the sinner truly know who it is whom he has lost and who in his inexpressible, unfathomable mercy calls him back to his heart. There is no salvation apart from this inner knowledge and conviction, for the simple reason that God takes the sinner far too seriously just to save him 'over his head'. But who is able to realise his true plight? Our sin consists in not being able to confess sincerely. For all sin is a lie. Who can make himself descend into the valley of the shadow of death and bear the burden of God's outcast? Only he whom the Father sent can do so, "My God, my God, why hast thou forsaken me?" (Mk. 15: 34), cries the dying Saviour on the cross. He cries it on behalf of us all. One with us, bearing our sin, he communicates to us the responsible realisation and true conviction of our deadly predicament. One with us, he rises from death, communicating to us the joyous fact of our forgiveness and acceptance with God. One with us, the risen Lord gives us his Spirit, in order that we may with a reconciled conscience call on God as our Father and pray him to hallow his name in us through our constant regeneration in a life and death struggle with our sin.

The new life which Christ imparts to us with his death and resurrection provides the prayer for the hallowing of the Name with a background of reality that we believe is required for worshipping God in spirit and in truth.

6

I HAVE tried to sketch the fundamental differences between Christianity and Judaism. The analysis of the Messianic titles is not included in my present purpose. The popular idea that the chief difference between the two religions is that Christians believe that the Messiah has already come, while Jews believe that he or the Messianic kingdom have not yet come, is fraught with ambiguity. I agree with S. R. Johnson's assertion that 'Jesus is greater than any of the titles applied to him'.[26]

Nor is it within the scope of this study to delineate the differences in the respective ideas of the kingdom, understood as final consummation; but a few remarks may serve to underline what has been said about the hallowing of the name. For the two respective petitions follow one another not only in the Lord's Prayer but also in synagogal prayer.

That the world is not yet redeemed constitutes an old and ever repeated Jewish argument against the Christian faith. War and strife, racial and economic oppression still desecrate God's creation. People go on sinning as if nothing had happened, and the Christian sinning is no more but rather definitely less excusable than Jewish sinning.

Furthermore, the Old and the New Testaments promise a cosmic redemption (e.g. Is. 11: 6-9; Hab. 2: 14; Rom. 8: 18-25; Eph. 1: 9 f.). Nothing of it has materialised as yet. Where is then the promised kingdom? What about Christ's promise to bring in the kingdom?

The answer to this widely-held objection requires a clean break with Christian self-righteousness. Israel is the paradigmatic people, that is the pattern for the history of all nations. The proper typological understanding of the Old Testament sees in the history of the Church the same judgments which Israel's prophets pronounced upon their own people. It would be an intolerable presumption on the part of the Church to claim that the prophets' uncompromising message of death referred only to Israel of old and not to herself too. The horrid pretension of being better than the Jews involves the forfeiture of our standing as God's children. "The Lord has a controversy with his people," Jews and Christians alike (Hos. 4: 1; Mic. 6: 2). "For the time has come for judgment to begin with the household of God" (1 Pet. 4: 17).

What is then the advantage of the Church? It is that we are privileged to hallow the name of God who has a controversy with us, as his active witnesses against ourselves. If everything that is has a purpose, then the 'purpose' of sin consists in its being constantly exposed in all its hideousness till it is conquered and destroyed. Physically, parents beget their children. Historically and sociologically, every man is to a large extent influenced by the past and by his present environment. Spiritually the natural order is reversed. The child must beget his forbears by continuing as God's witness in God's controversy with them in which they either refused to take their proper place, or at the best, did no more than was required of them in God's lenient forbearance. The same holds of powerful influences, good ones that must be rendered less and less ambiguous, evil ones that must be more and more unambiguously overcome. We people seldom realise how close we all are to one another. Our witness for God and against ourselves we can only bear in the togetherness of all generations from 'Adam' to the close of the Age. For rendering *our testimony* for God and *against ourselves* we entirely depend on Christ who with his death and resurrection effected what the Law could not affect, to set us against ourselves and thus deliver us from ourselves.

Throughout this Age our hallowing of the Name can be regarded only an incipient. Figuratively speaking, the history of God's people is like the assembling of a large orchestra against the Day when the Conductor will direct it in public. Till then it is our duty to tune our instruments, to practise, to invite our prospective fellow musicians to join us. The orchestra can only start performing the eternal symphony of the love of God once all members needed to play the score have gathered. Then the Son of God will raise his baton.

To ask why his first and his second coming do not coincide is to presume knowledge of the full score which is known to the Father only (Mt. 24: 36). The way the argument from the delay of the Parousia (Christ's return in glory at the end of the present age) is often raised qualifies as rationalism no less alien to the Jewish than to the Christian inheritance. Sometimes the argument is raised with a grin. Let me meet it in the simplest Jewish, Old Testament terms: "So Jacob served seven years for Rachel, and they seemed to him but a few days because of the love he had for her" (Gen. 29: 20).

For in waiting for the eternal kingdom we are already now anticipating its full realisation. The Holy Spirit (God as his own 'motive power', giving himself to those who are in Christ) fills all who in weakness and bitter struggle with themselves have begun to hallow the Father's name with a radiant hope through which the coming kingdom becomes a present reality. By hope we are walking already now in the outskirts of the New Jerusalem. The rays of the heavenly light that fill the city of God shine in our hearts. In offering the petition for the hallowing of the Name, followed by those for the coming of the Kingdom and the doing of the Will, we enjoy already now a sweet foretaste of the ultimate, world-wide redemption, when the power of Christ's sacrifice will be imparted to every creature according to its station, and everything that breathes, even everything that is, will hallow the Name. (Read Ps. 148).

Already now we call on God as his children, his new creation. We know for certain that we cannot hallow his name. For we know for certain that our minds are not bent on serving and glorifying God but rather on glorifying ourselves and serving our own petty ends. How do we know? Not from our self-understanding, nor by the application of psychological gimmicks. We know it through faith in the Son of God who died for us. That in the Father's judgment the Son had to die proves our need of radical transformation from rebels to children of God. He who died and rose for us is the Victor over us, which we are called to prove with our constant renewal till we breathe our last.

For this proof which in being presently tendered makes the glory of God a blissful presence we depend in every hour on the strength which Christ supplies. Our joyful conviction of faith that in Christ God is with us (Immanuel) implies our faith in the deity of Christ. He who with his mighty and loving presence enlivens countless people all over the world, simultaneously, is God. Quite consistently, the deity of Christ was acknowledged already in the worship of the primitive Church. This accords with his self-testimony as adduced earlier in this study.

Faith in the deity of Jesus is intolerable to Judaism. In the words of a contemporary scholar that may be fairly regarded as typical; 'it blurs the line of demarcation between God and man, and contradicts strict transcendent monotheism, that fundamental tenet of the Jewish creed'.[27]

Now we Christians consider ourselves monotheists, even strict monotheists; we translate *monos* by 'only', 'sole', 'exclusive', and not by 'one'. We believe in God alone who revealed himself to the fathers, to Moses and the prophets, and finally and totally in the word, the work, the person of Jesus Christ. In worshipping this God alone, we strictly reject the worship of the numeral 'one'. Classical Christian theologians (Gregory of Nyssa, Peter Lombard) averred that the three in the doctrine of the Trinity are not to be numbered.[28] And a contemporary Jewish historian of religion, who I feel sure, believes neither in the Incarnation nor in the Trinity, writes: 'It is not a question of number that distinguishes the Israelite idea of God . . . It is not an arithmetical diminution of the number of gods, but a new religious category that is involved'.[29]

What about 'transcendent monotheism'? The fact that there is no biblical Hebrew word for transcendence does not prove anything. There is no word for conscience either yet the conscience is everywhere in the Bible. But is there anything in the Old Testament that if translated into our conceptual terms can be taken for an assertion of divine transcendence? Assertions to this effect are in Philo and later in Moses Maimonides, but not in the Old Testament. According to G. F. Moore[30] the idea was unknown in Palestinian Judaism at the time of Christ and during the following centuries.

The prohibitions in the Decalogue concerning the worship of other gods and the making of idols involve no doctrine of transcendence, but rather one of incomparable, absolute superiority, and the demands that follow from its revelation in Israel's incipient history. God is not transcendent but highly exalted in the majesty of his holiness, in his heavenly mercy:

"Who is like the Lord our God,
   who is seated on high,
who looks far down
   upon the heavens and the earth?
He raises the poor from the dust,
   and lifts the needy from the ash heap" (Ps. 113: 5 ff.; Cp. Ps. 138: 6).

God can therefore be implored to "bow the heavens and come down" to deliver his servants (Ps. 144: 5. Cp. Is. 64: 1-3). He did come down in Jesus Christ. The objection that that 'contradicts strict monotheism' and 'blurs the line of demarcation between God and man' will not greatly impress him.

No doubt, the New Testament goes far beyond the Old. In whatever manner the Servant Song (Is. 52: 13 to 53: 12) is interpreted, he on whom "the Lord has laid the iniquity of us all", who "poured out his soul to death" as "he bore the sin of many" to see his life-and-death-work triumphantly vindicated is undoubtedly a human agent. In the light of the New Testament revelation we confess and adore the merciful Lord who did not will to pass on the cup of redemptive suffering to a merely human agent. He drank it himself. "God was in Christ, reconciling the world to himself" (2 Cor. 5: 19). Without this confession we Christians would indeed break away from biblical monotheism in separating the Redeemer from God.

Though faith in the deity of the Suffering Servant is beyond the Old Testament it does not contradict it. It is quite in line with God's involvement in the human predicament, his 'pathos' shared by the prophets, as it has been forcefully described by the contemporary Jewish theologian Abraham Heschel.

In Christ God has become our servant. Faith in Christ is *fellowship* with Christ; therefore it means infinitely more than the use of the Servant as an instrument. We rejoice in his eternal presence with us. The fact that without him we can do nothing but sin is not a matter of regret. The Christian no longer desires to go it alone. Even if he could—*posito sed non concesso*—hallow the Father's name unaided he would not avail himself of it. I do not want to be 'free' if that separates me from Christ's blest presence. I want to be free with him, in him. The relation of the grace of Christ and Christian freedom must not be described in the manner of a parallelogram of forces where different pulls or pushes are integrated. The two cannot be opposed to one another but constitute an indivisible unit as Paul triumphantly asserts: "It is no longer I who live, but Christ who lives in me; and the life I now live in the flesh I live by faith in the Son of God, who loved me and gave himself for me" (Gal. 2: 20). Christ hallows the Father's name in us and we hallow the Father's name in him.

7

IT sometimes happens that people who widely disagree on some fundamental point politely terminate their debate with the trite statement: 'We agree on ultimate aims though we differ in point of method'. Well, Christians and Jews do not agree on the hallowing of the Name as their central concern yet their difference is not one of method. We Christians must insist that we have no 'method' for responding to the divine call. We believe in One who pronounced his blessing upon the poor, the sorrowful, the hungry and thirsty. We praise the Father that the Son's blessing has proved effective. And we invite all our fellow men, Jews and Gentiles, to share our poverty in order that they too might share the inexhaustible riches of God's free gift in Christ.

We must invite the Jewish people. For we pray for them, and unless we act on our prayers our sincerity remains subject to doubt. What are the prospects for their response to our invitation? I will limit my remarks to the American scene.

Although the Jews in this country are in a far better position than in many other countries they will never forget their long history of suffering. Even if the individual is not conscious of it, the memory is kept. I have not met any Jew anywhere who did not bear this memory, deep down in his soul.

The Jews therefore would listen more readily to what we must tell them if they saw that the Church is also a suffering community, pilgrims and strangers in the signal sense of being marked by the sufferings of Christ.

Are the Churches of Christ in America clearly conscious of their own tribulation as Churches? If we are spared persecution for confessing the name of Christ—and to ask for persecution is perverse though it may come unasked for—do we in our hearts suffer from the worldliness of the world around us? Or do we try to outdo it in preaching a childish worldliness, allegedly informed by thinkers like Karl Barth and Dietrich Bonhoeffer? Do we—and here the primary emphasis must always be placed—suffer from our own worldliness as individuals and as a Church? Is the last prayer in the New Testament, "Come, Lord Jesus!" (Rev. 22: 20) also our prayer?

If it is, is its thrust borne out by a faith that discerns the sum total of our experiences with ourselves with the whole present Age? The deeper and the more real the conviction grows that nourishes this prayer, the more our Jewish brothers and sisters will realise what unites us. Consequently, they will be prepared for the challenge of that which separates them from us. Both are necessary for their receiving the Divine revelation that Jesus Christ "is our peace who has made us both one . . . that he might reconcile us both to God in one body through the cross" (Eph. 2: 14, 16).

Notes

1. E. F. Scott, *The Lord's Prayer*, 1951.
2. E. Lohmeyer, *Das Vaterunser*, 1946.
3. *The Torah*, Jewish Publications Society of America, 1962.
4. G. F. Moore, *Judaism in the First Century of the Christian Era*, 1950, Vol. 2. 202.
5. *ibid.* 201-11.
6. *ibid.* 205.
7. *ibid.* 103, note 2. See Strack-Billerbeck, *Kommentar zum NT aus Talmud und Midrasch*, 1922, Vol. 2, 413.
8. Moore, 2. 101.
9. *ibid.* 103 f.   Strack-Billerbeck, 1. 412 f.
10. Tertullian, *De Oratione*, ch. 3.   Cyprian, *De Oratione Dominica*, ch. 12. Augustine, *De Sermone Dominica in Monte*, closely followed by Luther in *Minor Catechism*.
11. Strack-Billerbeck, 1. 414 ff.   Moore, 2. 105 f.
12. Quoted from Moore, Vols. 2, 111.
13. G. von Rad, *Theologie des Alten Testaments*, 1960, Vol. 2. 243.
14. Moore, 1. 507-34.
15. J. Pedersen, *Israel*, 1959, Vol. 1. 104 f.
16. Von Rad, *loc. cit.*, 261.
17. *ibid.* 260.
18-24. E. Lohmeyer, *Das Vaterunser*, 1951, 23-37.
25. Moore, 2. 205.
26. 'Christ' in *Interpreter's Dictionary*, 1962, Vol. 1. 565.
27. H. J. Schoeps, *Paul, The Theology of the Apostle in the Light of Jewish Religious History*, 1961, p. 158.
28. See the writer's article in the *Hartford Quarterly*, 3. 1. 37-41 (1962).
29. Y. Kaufmann, *The Religion of Israel*, 1960, p. 226 f.
30. Moore, *loc. cit.*, 1. 417, 423 ff.

8. God's Fifth Columnist

A Dialogue in Four Parts

*In remembrance of Søren Kierkegaard
with profound respect
and never ending gratitude*

Author's Preface

IN INTRODUCING THIS DIALOGUE, I feel reminded of another dialogue, which is not fictitious.

Let me quote from it:

Christ: For this I was born, and for this I have come into the world, to bear witness to the truth. Everyone who is of the truth hears my voice.

Pilate: What is truth?

The records give no indication to the effect that Pilate afterwards changed his position—if you call it a position.

Suppose he had subjected Christ's declaration to a mere logical analysis he might have arrived at an answer to his question. For according to this declaration truth is what is attested, expressed in a confession. The testimony is given with the life of the witness.

That conclusion is simple, but Pilate so far as we know never drew it. It seems that more than mere logic is required in order to proceed logically.

That is a remarkable fact. I believe it is also a remarkable commentary on the Saviour's declaration.

God's Fifth Columnist

A Dialogue

PART I   A Tentative Definition

Claimant⎫
            ⎬ *Friends*
Tester   ⎭

The scene is at Claimant's home.

C   And when bad comes to worse?

T   Then we are left with this Government.

C   And with those its critics.

T   [*after interval*]   We two have very much in common.   Yet in our present discussion the only point of agreement seems to be . . .

C   That we are both angry.

T   [*laughs*]   What conclusions can we draw from those common premises?

C   Well, I don't know . . . Or rather, there is one, if you call it a conclusion.   You may also call it a suggestion.   It has been at the back of my mind during the last part of our heated discussion.

T   I would like to hear your suggestion.

C   Let us stop criticising God.

T   What did you say?

C   I said we should stop criticising God.

T   But who did that?

C   We both.

T   I cannot understand you.   During our whole talk the name of God was not at all mentioned.

C   Still he is the real object of our foolish anger.

T   [*after a few moments*]   I wouldn't deny that it is a foolish thing to get as angry as I am.   But as to the rest of what you say . . . that sounds rather paradoxical.

C   Anger as such is not always foolish, and—speaking for myself —I think I can justify my strong reaction against those self-styled politicians who slander the Government to make a career for themselves.   Yet there is something else in my anger which perverts it, and that points in the direction I have indicated.

T I need not tell you again that the objects of *my* anger are quite different. I must resent that irresponsible unwillingness on the part of our fumbling leaders to face reality. Yet I agree with you in that there is something in my reaction I can justify and something else I cannot. So far so bad. But as to your theological implications, I cannot follow you . . . not this time, at least.

C It exasperates me that that could happen at all and that it could happen to a nation to which I belong. In reacting against it I react against him who must have let it happen.

T That's too far fetched. I mean your conclusion. The presence of selfish motives I must admit. Our political confusion aggravates me not so much because it is a confusion, but because in some way it threatens my own well-being.

C I don't know whether I am entitled to this remark. Yet I feel tempted to pay you back in your own coin. It is your present statement that seems to me far fetched.

T [*laughing*] I'll be glad if you can prove that. For in this case I shall be exonerated from the charge of impure motives.

C Who knows? Suppose your motives are of a much nobler kind than you indicated. That would not necessarily exonerate you or us, for that matter. Or are you quite sure it would?

T Go ahead.

C Let us try a more beautiful explanation of our anger. Actual experiences clash with our ideas about what this world in general and this nation in particular ought to be. Frustrated idealism. Would that justify our reaction?

T [*after a moment of reflection*] It wouldn't. For idealistic attitudes like this one can still harbour lots of selfish motives. The world should have been constructed in greater conformity to my demands. Even if my demands can be styled altruistic it is not their altruistic nature which makes their frustration so provocative to me. It is rather the fact that they are *my* demands. For even the nobler self is big with a greedy thirst for aggrandisement. The moment we realise that we cannot have our own way our pride is hit and explodes with anger.

C You will now agree that I did not intend exculpating ourselves. Accusing oneself of trivial, egoistic motives is sometimes an ingenious device . . .

T To keep the more painful aspects of our reactions at bay.

You are right. Claimant, I must not go on with my artifices
. . . Or do I hear you say that I promised too much?

C I said nothing.

T To prove my new-fangled improvement I shall attack some
more of my monsters. Here is another, moral cowardice.
Instead of facing that political jumble with a sober and, for that
matter, no less sensitive mind, one flies—or shall I say flees—into
a passion.

C And the object of our passion?

T I know what you are driving at, and I appreciate your sticking to your point. You have not, however, succeeded in
making it clear to me.

C So let me try further. Here is still another of the painful
aspects to which you referred, self-righteousness. The just
indignation of a high-principled advertiser . . . The clamorous
voice of a staunch champion, swollen with strong persuasions.
We know that well, that is, with others.

T We sieved gnats and swallowed camels . . . Yet does that
bear out your contention?

C All self-righteousness contains a tactical element. 'Keeping
at bay,' you said. What do we keep at bay? I believe it is
not only our own state of mind. To make this limitation means,
in my opinion, tearing the whole picture asunder, rather arbitrarily
as if man were only concerned with himself. But he isn't. There
is one who besieges us, and against whom our inflated hearts sally
forth. Of course, only with our arguments. In attempting to
prove ourselves right, we want to prove him wrong, establishing
ourselves in the citadel of our presumptuous ego.

T [*after a while*] It may seem shallow to contradict you.
What you said impresses me. I can appropriate it so long
as I take it poetically or oratorically, and that in the best interpretation of the term. But you mean to talk prose. Then, however,
I must ask you for the sources of your knowledge concerning that
particular relation to God. Moreover, it is not the same thing to
call self-righteousness a sin against God, the worst of all sins—and
to make the assertion that he and I behave like partners in a talk.

C He may be humble enough and loving to accept this role.

T He may be humble enough to appear in human shape this
very moment. Yet he didn't do it. The question is not one
of possibilities but of facts. Now there are facts and facts. A

good number of them can be ascertained by observation and experiment. You will not possibly claim that your thesis refers to facts of that order.

C   We are not engaged in natural research just now.

T   All right. There are different sets of facts which we know only from other people's testimony. Nevertheless, we have accurate methods of checking on them.

C   I guess we are not working on one another's biographies.

T   Then there are facts and events that can be properly approached by religious faith only. I cannot suppose you to claim for your present thesis the impelling urgency of a Divine revelation. In that case I should have to ask you for your credentials. If that is out of the question, then, I must admit I cannot understand the meaning of your statement, its logical place and intent.

C   Are you certain that your alternatives are comprehensive enough to embrace the whole width of our approach to what is real?

T   [after interval] Well, there can be inferences drawn from accepted facts. That's, of course, a matter of Logic.

C   If I understand my own words they mean more than mere inferences.

T   That put me at my wit's end. I do not wish to be prejudiced. Yet if you want to make your point clear to me you will have to change your method. Mere self-analysis seems not to be enough. Look at what we have registered till now: Primitive egoism, moral cowardice, self-righteousness, greedy and imperialistic idealism. I am sure, several more items of that kind could be added to our list. Suppose we had gone through all of them. Would that help me or anybody else to understand your proposition that our foolish anger is immediately directed against God?

C   I am sorry I cannot promise you to change my method. I rather feel like extending it.

T   In what direction?

C   Going back behind our anger.

T   Depth psychology?

C   No. Our task is simpler and more serious. The depth—if you call it that way—which opens before my mind is being forced open by the unsolicited activities of my conscience rather than by the deliberate applications of scientific methods of introspection.

T If that is your particular approach I must ask you whether conscience can be turned into a source of knowledge. I may be wrong, but in my opinion conscience only reinforces what we already know. It does not add to its content. The reason seems to be that the range it covers is what we call ethical. I am a bit afraid you are going to trespass on what is beyond this range.

C Would you really deny that conscience can teach?

T You may use this word so long as it does not mean enlarging our knowledge of facts.

C If my conscience makes me alert to the fact that a man I resent and wish to ignore is a living person like me, does it not teach me a very important lesson?

T In this interpretation I should accept the term.

C Again if my conscience urges it on me that one I have relegated to the background of my mind yet only in order to go on arguing with him there, is, in fact, the living God—would you not call this a most serious lesson?

T I would if that happened. But did it? As yet I am not aware of any other immediate object of my anger beside those folks whom each of us respectively blames for our political mess.

C Taken as mere objects of our anger, they are no real people. They are somebody else's whipping boys, grimacing substitutes we have appointed to hide from our conscience the one with whom we are really at odds.

T You mean to say that we are not really reacting against them?

C We react against them chiefly because they reveal to us our insecurity, our vulnerability, our weakness, our shame. It is not they as persons against whom we turn; it is what they reveal. The lesson they are destined to teach us—much against their own will—we refuse to accept. In rejecting it, we cry out against the instruments the Teacher uses. We cry out against them, but we mean the Teacher. For what he is going to teach us, and the way he is doing it—that hurts.

T We are being humbled. So far I agree. As to the rest I still wonder.

C To suffer humiliation means being brought low. Now what is the original position from which one is brought low?

T Pride.

C Let us be more specific. *You* put the blame for this jumble
on our Government. *I* find fault with the insidious under-
mining of public morale by means of intimidation and calumny.
We are both shocked. In trying to get over our shock, we make
different groups of people responsible for the events which have
caused it. I call this a stratagem of diversion. We want to keep
ourselves safe from acknowledging who it is with whom we are at
war, and who has just now inflicted another defeat on us. We
sense our defeat; we complain about it; we protest against it, but
in a way that veils the true nature of battle and defeat. Yet veil
it we must so long as we are unwilling to learn our lesson.

T Do you imply that my refusal to agree with you is part of
that same stratagem?

C When I said WE I meant WE. Laying the fault at your
door, would be unfair and lead nowhere. Let us consider
the nature of the attack. The fact of our being shocked proves
that it came suddenly. For otherwise we should have reacted in
a different way.

T To that I agree. Our feeling of humiliation was something
we had not anticipated. That accounts for the vehemence
of our reaction. We simply did not realise what mess we were in
until the events compelled us.

C To what?

T As you said before, to recognising our insecurity, our vulnerability.

C Now is it likely for a man to be shocked by such an experience unless he had previously made the claim . . . ?

T Of being safe and strong and immune from attack. Honestly
speaking, I am not conscious of having made such a claim.

C Nor am I.

T Raising such a claim would run counter to common sense.

C And its frustration could not have produced that particular
reaction. We were shocked and reacted passionately not
because we discovered having misjudged our strength, but
rather . . .

T Because our pride was hit. What about your claim then?

C It is of quite a different nature. When I was shocked it was
not because I learned that I was less safe than I had thought
to be. The lesson was far more humiliating. It was brought home
to me that I am less safe than I thought I deserved to be. *That*

made me angry.   I ought not to be treated this way.   It's unfair.
Finding myself weak and vulnerable is not congenial to me.
Insecurity has no legitimate demand to make on such a glorious
being as I.   That's the claim I raised, and for which my conscience
struck me when the public events revealed its futility.

T   That rebuke we resented.   And since we would not admit
     rebelling against our conscience we used people connected
with the revealing events as our scapegoats.   They are guilty of
my pride.

C   It all goes back to our self-appraisal.   For we think of our-
     selves in terms of beings of a higher rank than we actually
hold.   It is not the unpleasant sight itself against which we protest;
it is the affront I must suffer in being presented with it: 'That such
things can happen to *me* . . . That *I* have to put up with them . . .
For even if I can do something about them, the fact that they happened is an offence.   I had not been consulted before!'   Well,
those things happen to us just because we are people.   Reality
itself continually confounds our claim . . .

T   To be more than people.   That seems to be at the root of
     all our pride.   Man always wants to be more or, at least to
seem to be more than he actually is.

C   How much more?   Just a bit?

T   Quite a bit, I should say.

C   Aspiring to the status of dynamic leader, dictator, super-
     man?

T   That's ridiculous.

C   What we actually presume to be is still more ridiculous
     though it is no laughing matter.

T   What would you say it is?

C   To be gods ourselves.   That makes us resent every forceful
     reminder of our humanity.   That makes us clash with God.
For God resists our presumption.   He does not do it because he
felt insulted like a man whose rank in society is challenged.   Such
stupid and blasphemous thoughts can we harbour only so long as
we have no idea of what the glory of God is. The glory of God is the
truth.   As for us, we can never be helped, we can never be saved
unless we acknowledge the truth which we are denying with our
claim for Divinity.   There is no compromise between the truth to
be expressed by the heart's praise of its Creator—and self's irreverent grasp at the worship that is due to God alone.   So long as we

worship ourselves we deny the truth and contradict God. The rest is a constant manoeuvring to keep the truth from our sight, arguing with God all the time. When we lashed out against the whipping boys we meant him. 'Let us stop criticising God,' I said before. 'Let us stop contradicting him,' we better say now.

T [*after interval*] Suppose for a moment that you are right. Why do we then argue with God in such a twisted manner?

C You cannot argue with God except in a twisted manner.

T Very true, but how mysterious! If our inner attitude toward God is as you said—why do we supply those whipping boys? Why do we not admit reacting against him? Why do we hide the true object of our anger? Not that we try hiding it from God's knowledge—that I could understand in a pinch—but why do we hide it from ourselves? Why must we always argue with ourselves?

C The reason is that we are made in God's image.

T What was that?

C The image of God in us does not prevent us from doing wrong. It does, however, prevent us from doing wrong without offering an excuse for it. We must constantly justify our desires, thoughts and actions, never admitting that black is black, but calling it white or grey at least. Even the most callous ideology that arose in our lifetime had to assume a pose of heroism, for instance: Another set of deceived deceivers, and a pretty vocal one nowadays, congratulate themselves upon their profound realism which shows them in conformity to the very core of history as laid open by their splendid scientific dialectics. Whatever the actual standards are in a specific case, there must be standards. The fact that we cannot help being standard-bearers shows the image of God working in us. A man may blaspheme God or deny his existence altogether, but then he does it in the name of intellectual honesty, moral courage or as an expression of noble sympathy with human suffering and genuine protest against superstition. Every idolator in prostrating himself before his nasty or threadbare idol, testifies that man is by nature a worshipper.

T What you said appeals to me and bewilders me, at the same time. So let me try to digest it in formulating my possible doubts. So far as I can see you have made three points. The first concerned rationalisation. The fact itself is undeniable though one might perhaps ask whether you do not claim for man a greater measure of rationality than can be admitted. Yet with that we better deal in discussing your second point. Here you asserted that in rationalising our wrong actions and attitudes we must always protest our conformity to some ultimate standard. Also that is very true so far as it goes. I wonder, however, whether it goes far enough to prove the general statements about human nature you have drawn from it. Which leads me to your third and most important point. Suppose your statement that man is essentially an arguer could be maintained—that would not yet establish your main thesis. For your main thesis and the proper subject of our talk is that we are constantly arguing with God. What follows from your statement is only that we are arguing with our conscience. I am sure you do not intend defining conscience by calling it the voice of God plain and simple. You spoke of the image of God in man. I should be grateful if you could lead me to a clearer understanding of your use of this term. Now this is an awful tangle of problems, and I really do not see where to tackle it and how.

    C It would be quite natural to deal first with the logic of human excuses.

    T I agree, but would that not cause us a considerable digression?

    C I don't think so. For I believe it bears closely on our subject. Just remember that what I said was in reply to your questions why the true object of our anger was hidden from us and why, in arguing with God, we must always argue with ourselves. Therefore I suggest, first to strive for a clearer grasp of the nature of our excuses. If I understand you right you seem to have doubts as to the inner necessity of submitting to standards of justification.

    T Well, perhaps not. I can only say that when you spoke it struck me that nearly all of your illustrations were taken from current ideologies or other trends of thoughtlessness. Yet I wonder whether it holds good in all instances that man must make schemes to cover his shame. What about the liar, for instance, who freely admits that he told a lie?

    C Does he also freely admit being a liar?

    T Nobody likes being abused. I came across some folks who didn't feel embarrassed at all when being caught on a lie. I am sure you must have had a similar experience. Are they not exceptions to your rule?

H

C [*is silent*]

T Do you deny that there are such people?

C [*continues with his silence*]

T Why? . . . I know what you want to ask me with your silence.

C [*makes no reply*]

T You want to question me whether I am such a liar myself.

If I reply, I hope not, you will rejoin that a man must not cover up his lack of acumen by supplying hypothetical analyses of his neighbour's state of conscience. I can retort, however, that only a few moments ago you were referring to certain ideologies in which you have no share at all. Did you then draw on your own conscience exclusively?

C The difference is that those ideologies are preached everywhere, thus are subject to public examination and discussion. As to your hypothetical liar, however . . .

T Please let him write a book and give me your review.

C That might be unnecessary. In order to clarify my point I shall try acting the part of your liar. I admit then that in telling others about my successful career, I am not ashamed at all but rather proud of the devices I used.

T You even make a boast of them.

C Thus submitting to the standards of superior cleverness. Is not that also a kind of rationalisation?

T It is, but suppose you would not boast at all. Nor were your life career crowned with success. Nevertheless you would call your lies lies without feeling or expressing personal regret.

C In this case I should admit that from time to time I cannot help telling a lie. For I have to fit in with the World as it is. Think of the weeping wife at home and the crying kiddies, etc., etc. I thus solemnly protest my supreme allegiance to the sacred standards of duty, including, of course, reasonable self-preservation. It is these standards whose invocation protects me from acting like a rascal or more correctly from admitting that I have acted like a rascal.

T You did pretty well, Claimant, in covering up your lies. Still I have a few more questions up my sleeve. If you care to answer them please don't be squeamish. You know like me that there are people who really stick at nothing and don't seem to need any excuses. Why shouldn't you try making your point absolutely convincing by proving that they also must have standards to which they refer in their arguings?

C You seem already inclined to admit that even those folks cannot do without some arguing for the purposes of moral self-defence.

T Honestly speaking, I still wonder. For I have met some ones . . .

C What was your concern in trying to understand them? Was it one of profound sympathy with their moral debasement?

T Frankly, I felt a much more profound sympathy for their victims.

C And you needed an analysis of the victimiser's state of conscience in order to warn his possible victims.

T Not exactly. You won't presume, Claimant, that I am so ignorant of you as not to see through your schemes. You are just pleading for some more time in order to discover a definite refutation of my doubts. Now if you need time I shall keep silent till you have worked it out. Or else we may continue this talk a week from today. Let me only tell you one thing before we adjourn. To pronounce judgment upon the real motives behind the words and deeds of even the worst of all rascals, is no affair of mine. That I must leave entirely to his and mine Divine judge. Nor am I at present interested in the elaboration of psychological analyses. As to that, you made a pertinent remark a short time ago. We are dealing with matters of conscience which involve us in a way that permits neither of theorising nor of engineering. We are talking about our relationship to God. People we mention in this connection are not real people with their real needs and sins. They are constructed in order to let us check on our own thoughts and make clear to us where we stand or ought to stand. Of course, the construction must not be arbitrary. It must be saturated with life experience and expressive of the structure of reality. Yet we have to keep conscious, all the time, that what we have before us is a picture to illustrate a point and not a photo on a warrant. Otherwise, we should only have made one more contribution toward illustrating that finest claim of being more than people.

C Thank you, Tester. We are now on firm, common ground. There is no need for adjournment. What you want me to do is, I guess, to draw a sketch of a perfect cynic.

T That would be of great help, indeed.

C So let us take a public slanderer. Would that do?

T Remembering the hot debate we had before, I am afraid it
will be difficult for you to treat that figure only as a picture.
And don't forget, Claimant, you have no parliamentary immunity
to protect you in case I should talk.

C I am not afraid that you will talk since there was no dis-
agreement between us in this particular point. Besides, I
can claim some sort of immunity. I am given it by the purpose of
our discussion to which I shall have to stick. The character I am
going to delineate is and must remain of my own making. You
may be sure that I shall not supply any incident or concrete feature
from any public figure's life story as known to me or to anybody
else.

T All right. Go ahead, please.

C Our man cherishes great personal ambition: He wants to
climb up the ladder at any costs. He suspects, however, that
many of his glorious ambitions have been frustrated by those on
top. They are in his way; he plans to move them out of his way.
His plannings are interrupted by the veto of his conscience.
'What?', he retorts to his conscience, 'am I not a man of great
abilities? Yet I am constantly kept down by those fossilised,
idiotic grudgers. Just the other day, one of them was reported to
me saying that I wielded already far more influence than I deserved.
That's the way those fellows want to stifle the stirring of fresh
talent. Must that go unchallenged? Shall our public life be
permitted to freeze to death? Truly, the public interest itself constrains me to do something about those decadent fumblers!' Here,
his conscience protests against the way he plans to do something
about his opponents. In order to work out his reply our man
scratches the records, written and unwritten, for material. (Some
investigation in the public interest, he calls it.) There is, of course,
always enough material accessible. Armed with it he encounters
his conscience with a grin: 'What I always suspected is now an
established fact. Look at those most compromising connections.
Can it be doubted any longer that my enviers constitute a mortal
peril to the whole fabric of society? That must be stopped, and
immediately!' (What he will soon say or write in public he first
tells his conscience.) Yet his conscience is not stopped. It questions the motives of his hotly protested zeal for the public good.
Our man is, however, swift in repartee: 'Surely, I want to come on

top. Is there anything intrinsically wrong with that? Are there no noble aspirations? Those who are now on top are either criminals or imbeciles. A man like me is just the one needed to take the rudder in his hands. There is nobody else I know. Without my stepping in the boat must soon founder.' Until now the man has presented himself to his conscience (as he will soon do to the public) as a vigorous idealist and reformer. In the long run, however, he will have to give up that whole set of arguments. It will simply fade away, not like old soldiers but really. In the end, the man will literally not believe himself a word. By the way, that fading away of his whole stock of excuses is also the work of conscience, for conscience, in a marvellous manner, turns its own defeats into victories sombre as they are. Though it cannot prevent a slanderer from going about his business—it destroys his idealistic trappings one after another, if slowly yet surely. Our slanderer will thus end as a perfect cynic. Yet even then and particular in calling himself a cynic—in camera—he will have to make his cynicism palatable to himself and to his comrades in slander. He might cover it with the cloak of a mature wisdom that masters all the principles and details of the 'know how'. At the same time, however, he will get sentimental. With a tear in his eyes he will tell you that he was not always a cynic. 'No, no, there was a time when I was a blooming idealist just as you, my dear young friend, are now.' (He refers to the idealistic tricks he played on his conscience when he was younger.) 'My present Weltanschauung has been forced on me in a long process of growing disillusionment. Shall I regret it? In a way I do. Still it is a good thing to take this World for what it is worth.' It is in the name of a penetrating insight into the nature of the game, it is thus in the name of truth itself as he has managed to discover it that he will go on slandering honest people until he breathes his last.

 T Thank you, Claimant. Your construction has helped me a lot. By now it should not be too difficult to complete your argument by taking up the other case that was—shall I say on or under the threshold of my consciousness?—for I don't know when it appeared.

 C I feel you are prepared to tackle it yourself. What is your other case?

 T Nihilism.

 C So that's your turn, Tester. I have already talked enough,

T Not enough for me. But since I hope you will talk more
     this Sunday afternoon I shall take up the loose end of the
thread. There are several types of nihilism to be considered. If
we take the moral connotation of the term first, we may, for
instance, refer to those who do not only behave like beasts but also
have a Gospel of bestiality to offer. That Gospel betrays the
standards to which they recur in order to make arrangements with
their conscience. They worship the happy unconcern, the noble
virility, the ferocious grandeur which the animals seem to present
to them. (I personally think they misunderstand the animals
thoroughly. They simply envy them for not having a conscience
and out of their envy they try to emulate them. Yet an envier
never knows him whom he envies.)

C I think you are right, but what about those animal imitators
     who do not offer us a Gospel of bestiality? They just indulge
in their vices.

T Thank you for acting my part. Now my reply is that those
     last-mentioned lack the faculty or sometimes only the occa-
sion of becoming vocal. That makes no essential difference. Some
sort of arguing with themselves they must maintain, for even mad
people do that.

C All right. Let us examine some more categories.

T A very different sort of nihilists are those who think and act
     against a background of sheer despair. 'Do not move,' they
say. 'It is all the same.' The system of reference they use in their
gloomy monologues is created by an erratic block which once
invaded their life experience and which they have never succeeded
in integrating. Some leaden mass presses on them from the past,
suffocating all growth. If you argue with them you have to complete every one of their reasonings with what is their true argument:
'Since that once happened to me . . .'. It may sound very heartless
but I do feel that unless that had happened to them they would
have made something happen to a similar effect. For they need
that in order to justify their spiritual inertia. Again there are
others whose thrilling message strikes the key-note of death. The
words of Jesus, 'The truth will make you free,' they seem to apply
to death. According to their teaching death is the truth that will
make us free, the only source of light and sober resolution. I may
do them wrong by calling them nihilists. For the standard to
which they submit is not death but rather the grand heroism they

display in placing themselves boldly *vis-à-vis de rien.* With their
ostentation of freedom from everything they show themselves quite
intoxicated.   That is perhaps the reason why some of them furnish
their magniloquent discourses with a considerable amount of false
pathos.

C   Are you still constructing, Tester?

T   Reviewing books, dear, not talking about real people.

C   Some of those books have great merits of which you should
     not make light.

T   I hope I did not touch a weak spot with you.   Sort of scar.

C   Don't kid me.   Let us continue.   Do you take it for granted
     that there are no real nihilists?

T   I shouldn't say that.   We must never allow our constructions
     to close the horizon.   Remaining within the boundaries
drawn by our present purpose I should refer to at least one more
class.   For there are some who are genuinely and, if I may say
that, authentically sad and have ever been so.   The lyrical beauty
of their pensiveness makes an appeal.   It makes it to others and,
as I am sorry I must add, it does it also to themselves.   They could
not maintain their triste world view without enjoying, in their particular manner. the sweet melancholy of the dark lake, surrounded
by willows, to which they feel united in a life-long gaze.   The
sublime feelings they thus produce feed their dominating attitude
of self-assertion by remaining lonely and aloof.   They are not
trivial, they are deep going.   That is their manner of settling with
conscience.

C   I think we can now take up the second or rather the third
     point.

T   Not without my acknowledging that you have really proved
     the validity of your generalisations.

C   To that I must raise two objections.   First, if anything was
     proved or rather shown, it was done by you as well as by
me.   Second, I seriously doubt the validity of the term generalisa-
tions.

T   What other term would you suggest?

C   We furnished a number of illustrations in order to elucidate
     and appropriate a very concrete fact that has been before our
mind all the time.   We did not attempt to prove or disprove anything nor were we engaged in inductive or deductive transactions.
We need our intellect, of course.   But the logic that ruled our mind

was that of conscience. *'La logique du coeur,'* Pascal called it. That kind of logic cannot be used, it must be obeyed. I hope we were not altogether disobedient to its requirements.

T Did not Plato already practise this logic when he so clearly and penetratingly demonstrated that we can never just do what we will? There are certain barriers we cannot surmount. Those are not outward barriers. They are erected within us.

C They are the fundamental structures of our being. If we try to steal around them every success is in itself a failure. The greater the success the worse the failure. Or is there any more desperate failure than to fail oneself?

T Socrates once said that the worst of all is to deceive oneself. For then you must all the time keep a deceiver's company. I accept your correction, Claimant. However, I may have misunderstood my own previous questions, their true aim could only be my confrontation with the power of conscience. Otherwise, we might as well lecture to one another. By the by, Claimant, keep this remark in mind. We might have to come back to it later.

C We shall always have to. Everything one says or thinks one has to keep safe from oneself. Personally speaking, that is the only positive meaning I can attach to the term dialectical.

T I understand you. Now there is one question on my mind which I should like to see settled before we pass on to the next point. That is, if you don't mind.

C We must never feel being hurried. Didn't you just refer to Plato?

T In every excuse we make we use some standards or rather abuse them. It would thus appear that our whole moral system of reference is only for the purpose of assuaging our conscience. Yet that cannot be your opinion. Are there not good and necessary standards to which a man may honestly try living up? In other words: Is there not such a thing like a good conscience?

C There is, and I have but little sympathy with those who deny it. The question is, however, whether a man who really and unambiguously obeys his conscience regards his moral standards as fixed and rigid and flat ultimates. You spoke of honestly trying to live up to them. I do not wish to challenge your way of putting it. I am not fond of haggling over words. One thing, however, we must never forget, least of all now that fundamental issues are at stake. Are we going to submit to mere abstract standards or to the living God? Either God is himself *the* standard, then everything ought to be referred to him. Or else we lose sight of him, then have plenty of standards as illustrated before.

T Are there no standards under God?

C God claims our hearts in many ways. He calls us to himself in and through all the life-situations in which we are from one hour to another. Goodness, righteousness, mercy, sincerity, dedication, openness of heart and mind—those are only a few expressions for the response we owe to him, dependent on the concrete situation in which we are reached by his call. You may thus speak of standards or principles or norms or even absolutes and ultimates to which our attitudes and actions ought to conform. Apply whatever name you see fit. What matters is that those principles must not come in between God and us. Whenever this is the case they become idols. And that was certainly their function in the various illustrations we used. Now I am quite satisfied that your remarks have already carried us over to the last point you raised. For you asked whether it could be truly said that in arguing with our conscience we were arguing with God himself.

T You seem to maintain that the idolising of standards is sort of dodging the demand God makes on us. I still wonder whether this is not like shooting a god out of the machine. What you said about standards becoming idols may be quite true—and I believe it is true, being taken as an independent statement. I do not see, however, that our relatedness to our conscience does in itself express our relatedness to God—at least the kind of relatedness you seem to postulate. Let me take up an earlier remark. I hope you agree that calling conscience the voice of God is no more than an overstrained metaphor.

C Do you think that conscience has nothing to do with God?

T I should not say of anything that it is entirely unrelated to God.

C Would you say that conscience is related to God only so far as everything is related to him?

T Well . . . no. Conscience reinforces the Divine Commands, but that can only happen if we already know them. It has no creative function.

C Let us say more cautiously that the Commandments are given to our conscience, committed to it. Moreover, I do not suppose you would limit God's relation to us to Law-giving. Or is that the only way he converses with us?

T [*smiles*] If you are going to catechise me I am bound by my conscience to answer . . . No, it is not only and not chiefly the Law, it is the whole Divine Revelation which as you put it God has committed to our conscience.

C That was a good Protestant answer, but it needs some elucidation. Tell me, Tester, do you deny that not one sparrow will fall to the ground without our Father's will?

T How should I?

C God rules the World, part and parcel, at every moment. Has this no bearing on our present theme?

T I am not quite clear in what respect.

C Do you hear the voice of God only in studying the Bible or listening to a sermon? Or does God manifest himself through everything that is and happens? And does he do that only in a vague general manner? Or has he something definite to say to you, time and again? If all our life-situations are Divinely shaped, then we must confess that the content they offer means something to us and is destined to mean it, destined by God himself. There is a message everywhere.

T I do not deny that altogether though I could not subscribe to it without grave reservations. For there is some dangerous ambiguity about it. For though there is a message everywhere as you said, we can appropriate it only in the lights of Divine Revelation. Apart from Revelation, we are groping in the dark. As Calvin put it with a most profound simplicity, the Word of God in Scripture is the eye-glasses without which we see either nothing or but dim contours.

C That is perfectly true and perhaps one of the best-balanced statements made on this subject. Yet it does not imply that the running commentary on our whole life experience which the Bible mediates to us is destined for the nourishment of our intellectual life. When God speaks to us he does not intend to increase the sum total of knowledge that fills our brain. He speaks to our conscience. Recalling an expression you used a few moments ago, I should rather say that the Word of God reinforces, that is enlightens and strengthens our conscience instead of the reverse.

T I agree to that correction.

C Now whenever our conscience is actually reinforced by the Word and Spirit of God, then I believe it refers us to the mighty deeds of God in shaping every life situation and all the situation shows. Just take our disappointment with our shameful political situation. We have found fault with different groups of leaders. Yet notwithstanding their personal responsibility and ours, it would be cowardly to say that almighty God has only admitted those things to happen by way of concession. I call that cowardly because it is tantamount to offer apologies on his behalf. The Bible gives us quite a different picture of the Lord of history. For though in the Bible human causality is not denied and human responsibility emphasised far stronger than anywhere else, it yet proclaims God as the one who deals with us and with whom we have to do wherever we are and whatever happens. It is God who made Sennacherib and Nebuchadnezzar rods of his judgment. For quite similar purposes he has now appointed Mr. Easy Going, Mr. C. O. M. Placent, Mr. Graft Loyal, Mr. Heavy Inroad, Mr. Crafty McSmear and Mr. Change Forever, who are among the chief targets of our respective reaction of indignation. It is God who deals with us through these men, and his dealing with us means his dealing with our conscience. That we are now a bit frightened at the angry way we reacted to it we owe to the warnings we received from our conscience. I have never pretended that conscience is the voice of God. It is rather the echo in us of his voice. Or better: We are ourselves this echo. Our conscience is our own voice but as that it inculcates in us his messages to us here and now.

T Can you explain that further?

C The two most obvious features the conscience call offers are that it comes from within us yet, at the same time, stands over against us. It is both our friend and our enemy. Yet it dominates the picture in its latter capacity. For more often than not we receive its warnings and threats and judgments in a hostile attitude.

T It is not our enemy, but we are often its enemies.

C In a fight from which we can never disengage. For our conscience is not an organ of our mind which we could put to rest as we close our eyes or put stopples in our ears. It is more than part of ourselves. It pervades our whole being. It makes us what we are. Though it assails us sometimes like a man-at-arms we can never exist without it. We can never meet its attacks by means of counter-attack. Its voice does not suffer itself to be defied openly. We think and say many things, especially when we are in a passion, but the moment we should challenge our conscience, as it were determinedly, we had to break asunder. For our conscience is ourselves. We cannot live without trying to come to terms with ourselves from one moment to the next. Disobedience to the call of conscience can therefore take place only in the guise of previous or posterior arrangements. Hence the endless process of self-justification. We are vain and greedy and extremely inert. We are all this as individuals and as groups. We are it in a way no animal could ever exhibit. For our vanity is the exaltation of the individual or family or nation to Divine stature; our greed is the clutch at Divine power; our selfish and complacent inertia is the presumption of a deity, the aping of the Divine, 'I am that I am' by persistent human spiritlessness. Those aspirations cannot be maintained in broad daylight: therefore our existence as self-worshippers has all the ghostly unreality of somnambulism. God through the actual situation he posits calls us out of our slumber and evil dreams: Our conscience brings his call home to us. We refuse to obey but that never frankly. For then we had to part with our conscience which would mean losing ourselves altogether, tumbling into the bottomless pit of spiritual nothingness. Therefore we must disguise our disobedience. We make us idols which we invest with some stolen sparks of Divine splendour. Our loyalty to them shall prove our conscience wrong. Conscience should not interfere with our self-worship. For do we not own the Divine, are we not ourselves Divine? Our petty self seems enhanced, mightily, by our possessing the idol and being possessed of it. It makes not much difference which way it goes, for every idol-worship is worship of the enhanced self. Our sluggishness, cowardice and ruthless scheming we call profound realism, protesting that it is our concern for truth that compels us to face things as they are and act accordingly. That sort of truth is but a false picture of the truth. In doing obeisance to it, we pretend being in the truth. Or we effect some unselfish concern for others to legitimate our trivial personal ambitions. The standards of unselfishness by which we fancy ourselves lifted up are purloined from the goodness of God. In extolling them, we, their bearers, are likewise extolled and thus can be satisfied at being really Divine. Brutality covers itself with the idols of courage and strength of heart. It makes us partakers of the distorted image of greatness. Suicidal melancholy and wilful despair are counterfeits of Divine seriousness and profundity. To sum it up: In order to by-pass the Divine demands made on me through his works and my conscience I fabricate a false picture of God and by clinging to it as part of my enhanced self I take pains to persuade my conscience that this miserable self I am worshipping is truly God. Clad with a majesty and splendour it is deserving of all Divine worship.

T Can I take this for an exposition of the second Commandment in the Decalogue?

C It does not go far enough. For it does not cover the whole range of idolatry.

T Let us stop here for a moment and see where we stand. Our present digression (if it is one) started when I asked you why we must argue with God in a twisted manner. The reason for my question was that in all appearance we are not conscious of arguing with him at all. To this you reply that our ignorance is one we are constantly producing ourselves. For God has laid hold of our conscience and to part with my conscience would mean to part with myself. Thus we use stratagems. It belongs to the nature of a stratagem to be carried out in the dark. But once our conscience gets the better of us we know well enough what we have been doing all the time. Did I understand you so far?

C You did, though the picture of the stratagem does not carry us the whole way. For while a stratagem is executed in the dark, it must have been planned consciously previous to its execution.

T Right. When we dodge the call of conscience it is not only the execution but already the conception of our schemes that must shun the light. Therefore we are not conscious of our own manoeuvres as we are, for instance, conscious of a tooth-ache.

C Self-deception is real deception and immediately throws us into a night of black ignorance. 'Their foolish minds were darkened,' the apostle says.

T Now it is time to ask you to explain the use you made of the term, image of God. In going back to the source from which the term is taken, that is the book of Genesis, it seems to me to refer only to the excellency of man, his pre-eminence over the lower creatures which are subjected to his rule.

C In the last and ultimate stage of Divine Revelation God is called spirit. Taking this into account, the creation of man in the image of God means that he is a spiritual being.

T I have no particular objection although I remember one of our previous talks when you rather vehemently resented the flimsy use made of the word spiritual today.

C I have not changed my mood since then. I hope, however, that our considerations of the nature of conscience will lead us to a less ambiguous use of the word. The fact that man has a conscience and cannot help seeking to establish himself before its tribunal, reveals his spiritual nature. In bargaining with our conscience, we can never give up claiming the ground on which we are placed by having a conscience. The ultimate motives of our actions and designs, the whole direction of our life is thus related to the power of conscience. Does that not prove beyond contradiction that man liveth not by bread alone? He is made in the image of God, a spiritual being.

T I am glad that in speaking of the image of God, you are keeping clear of the cliffs to the right and to the left. If I understand you the image of God in man is a real and present perfection yet one we do not hold as it were in our hands. We do not possess it, it rather possesses us. It is not our personal perfection, but that of our organisation as spiritual beings. We are so made that we must repeat to ourselves the demands God makes on us. I should now like to ask you how you conceive of the nature of God's demands. For the call of God to which you referred is neither Law nor Gospel. At the same time, it is far too personal, too much of a direct challenge, to fit in with the rather vague and ambiguous idea of a so-called general revelation.

C Through everything that is and happens God speaks to me, calling me to himself. For God is so astonishingly humble as to seek my heart. To let myself be found by him, to respond to the truth of his universal language, means to worship him. For the worship of God is not a ceremonial prostration or sort of wheedling oneself into his favour. It is the heart's acknowledgement of one fact that forms the meaning of everything: his awful majesty and unsearchable goodness. Worship is a living testimony to the truth, 'the sacrifice of lips that confess his name'. Only in actually worshipping God, can I experience his goodness and majesty. Only by standing in the truth, can I commune with him. Only in community with him can I live. For man lives 'by every word that proceeds from the mouth of God'. To respond to his word, is the purpose for which we are made. And that is testified by the inescapable call of our conscience. For the ground on which we are placed by having a conscience, is the ground of truth.

T You mean to say that it is our own make-up that draws us to God.

C Though we constantly refuse being drawn to him.

T The fact of our having a conscience then means . . . one might say . . . something like a Divine counter-offensive to put down our rebellion.

C That is true, since the fall.

T It might look as if our Creator had parachuted an agent of his into the enemy camp, right into the depth of our own being.

C The picture is quite to the point.

T God's fifth columnist—how marvellous.

C And one without which we cannot exist. Our Creator has manifested his majestic power in planting a vigorous testimony against us rebels in the midst of our own hearts. Is that not truly Divine? God need not argue his cause. He can leave that to us. He lets us do his pleading ourselves. He treats us as spiritual beings. He does not push us from outside, he rules over us by means of ourselves. We are not the work of an engineer; we are roused to rouse ourselves. Thus our Creator has established his omnipotent power. For it is the true omnipotence of the spirit, to rule without moving a finger. God is the truth, and he rules over us in the power of truth.

T [*after interval of silence*] Yet we go on disowning the truth.

C Until we are stopped. That happens, too. Or did we not experience it again, today?

T Thank God, we did. For when we both called for his Divine majesty's whipping boys we suffered a blessed defeat.

C I can only repeat what you said: Thank God.

PART II   A Ride in the Subway

The scene is again at Claimant's home.
Tester is let in.   Exchange of greetings, coffee.

C   You look as if you had come by subway.
T   Yes, my car caught a cold.
C   Was it very bad?
T   Not so bad, I shall have it again tomorrow.
C   I am glad but I was rather thinking of your subway-ride.
T   It was no mere pleasure.
C   I can imagine it.   Such a long ride.
T   It made me think of you.
C   Did you want me to share your underground sufferings?
T   Not at all.   I want you to share the effect they had on my mind.
C   You must have been recompensed for your sufferings by a pretty stimulating experience.
T   You shall judge presently.   Well, to cut a long story short . . .
C   That's not necessary.   Tell me the whole of it.
T   If this is your desire I shall devise all the verbosity of a grand epic.
C   I promise you in return to interrupt you as often as I can.
T   That will help me greatly to concentrate on my narrative. Let me begin at Dirt Road Station.   Soon after I had entered the train all people were seated except myself.
C   How vicious of them.   It must have kept you busy.
T   Why busy?
C   Casting glances around all the time, pleading with people, suggesting that somebody must keep his promise to call on his friend who is living so near the next stop.
T   [*laughing*] I didn't do that all the time.
C   You did it only every half-minute before you knew the car was going to stop.
T   During the rest of the time I tried reading today's paper. When I thought I had finished it . . .
C   You took to some periodical.
T   I had none with me.
C   So you started thinking of me.
T   Not yet, not yet.   I thought of somebody else.   That inspired me to practise gymnastics.

C   What was that?

T   It was a very good exercise.

C   Exercise on the subway?   That's something new to me.

T   I learned it not so long ago from a very sweet and highly competent lady.   She is sort of my *magister elegantiarum*.

C   I guess who the lady is.   What I know of her competence makes me still more interested in your gymnastics.

T   It is the high art of standing in a subway car without ever touching a handle or a pole.

C   Were you leaning on some of the sitters?   That would have been a just punishment for their lack of human feelings . . .

T   Toward the friend they had promised to visit.   No, I am not that vindictive, otherwise I should have retaliated on you long since.

C   You know what keeps me at home today.   As to the future I promise improvement.

T   That gives me the strength and inspiration to continue my narrative.

C   So what did you do then?

T   What I said, I stood.

C   Aren't you a brave man?   How could you manage that?

T   For the time being this is a closely guarded family secret.

C   Hush, hush.   I see I must continue in my state of ignorance. One thing, however, I know.

T   What do *you* know?

C   Since this is no secret I can divulge it.   However, you managed to stand, you could not stand that kind of standing for more than ten minutes.

T   [*laughing*] Admitted.

C   What did you do afterwards?   I hope . . .

T   No, there was no empty seat available.

C   You misunderstood me.   I hoped for something else.

T   Not yet, not yet.   You will need a lot of patience.

C   You are a bad friend not to have thought of me.

T   You will forgive me if I tell you that I was hardly in a position to think at all.

C   I understand.   You were so tired from your good exercise.

T   Not *so* tired.   Something happened that paralysed my mind for quite a few minutes.

C   Something wrong with the train?

I

T　No.　The train was running as smoothly or roughly as ever.
Our car was stormed.

C　What do I hear?　A hold-up?

T　No.　A pack of progressively educated boys and girls rushed
in.

C　And the rest was not silence but quite on the contrary.

T　Let's say a promising life expression of their present stage
of sub-culture which must never be interfered with.　In order
to prove that they were no reactionaries most of the people in the
car smiled.　I smiled too.

C　And when you had finished smiling?

T　The teenagers continued with their intense cultural activities
for a goodly period of evolution.　At last, they left at the
Grand Pompous Station.

C　I hope you got a seat there.

T　Not I.　It would not have made much difference though.
For at that stop every imaginable spot of the car was immediately occupied by a crowd of Harpies.

C　Poor man.　What tribe of Harpies?　Peanut or chewing
gum?

T　Both kinds were represented.　Though that was not the
characteristic feature of the tribe.　You must take a course
in twentieth century mythology.

C　Did they return from a political convention?

T　A near miss.　They were ex-movie-attenders who with their
genial gestures and cheerful hullabaloo reproduced the western they had just enjoyed.

C　How many casualties?

T　Count the stars in the sky.

C　I hope none of the by-standers was shot dead.

T　That was what I feared.　Still the actors took some considerations.　So nothing particular happened, except one or
two incidents I must mention for the sake of what follows in the
story.　There was a tall young couple which I first took for profes-
sional acrobats.　I was, however, wrong as you shall soon discover.
During the preceding movie performance those two must have
devoted a most serious study to various positions in kissing and
hugging.　In the car, they soon started practising what they had
learned.　Their performance offered the peculiarly interesting
feature of being given in jumping.　On a sudden, they landed on

both my feet. For a moment I must have looked angry. The man, rightly astonished, asked me whether something was wrong. What else could I do but give a wry smile? The man replied in kind and that so obligingly that he had almost reconciled me to my plight had it not been for that terrible heat in the car. Then I thought, however, that in case I had been sitting the bottom of my trousers would probably have been burned to ashes.

    C   You really made the best of it. Did you give some warning to your sitting travel companions?

    T   I could neither see any of them nor make my voice heard. The only thing I could do was peeping between the shoulders of that couple of art students.

    C   To be captured by a wonderful landscape. I mean on the wall. There were green pastures with grazing cows, and below them some most comfortable and glorious promise with a philanthropic invitation to act on it.

    T   In principle you are right. In fact, it was not a cow but a human face, or rather two pictures of the same face. The one to the left looked simply appalling, the other radiant and perfectly reconciled to God and World. I understood that some great and decisive event must have turned that fellow-citizen's entire destiny.

    C   Things like these really happen, that is if people are bright enough to heed the lesson. Sometimes it is a razor blade, sometimes a deodorant or a brand of liquor.

    T   I kept wondering what it was, since my new friends obstructed my view of the printed message. After some minutes of painful suspense they fortunately decided to take a jump on somebody else's feet. During that moment the view opened, and with a quick glance I could satisfy my curiosity. That is to say part of it, for before I had finished reading the legend the couple came back again. Still, what I saw impressed me.

    C   That must have been something really important, for I know your critical mind. How did this Sunday afternoon text run?

    T   'IT'S YOUR THROAT,' it said. It sounded in my ears like a deep sonorous voice with an undertone of accusation. There was no denial. For it was indeed my throat. I had felt it for some time though unconsciously. Now, however, I knew. All that stuffy air in the car had settled on my throat, and that was the reason why I was feeling so miserable. Yes, it was my throat.

While I could not help admitting it, I pondered over the meaning of the explanatory indictment. Was the wretched face that kept staring at me a true picture of my own derelict self? In asking the question, I detected some sense of guilt which I must have been harbouring for some time. Had I done something amiss? Had I shirked duty? Perhaps it was only forgetfulness though even that would not leave me innocent, facing my hideous counterpart and hearing that authoritative voice. Oh that voice! It simply did not let me pass. It compelled me to go on with my heart-searching . . . Yes, I must have missed taking something along with me. Or perhaps I should have bought it before I walked down the subway stairs. Just when that idea crossed my mind, the happy pair, having chosen another victim, jumped again. Another glance and I knew the cause of all my troubles. 'REDEMPTIVE WILL DO IT,' so I read, and since, for some reason I was in no mood to look for, the couple did not swing back immediately, I was able to listen to the close of my subway Gospel text. 'AT YOUR NEXT DRUGSTORE,' it concluded. Automatically, I looked up again and beheld the transfigured face at the right. At this moment the train stopped at Nevergreen Hill where I had to change for the local. The local train was already waiting and nearly empty, but I manfully resisted the allurement. For I knew that I was due to make amends and the quicker the better. 'AT YOUR NEXT DRUGSTORE,' thus it had been proclaimed to me with an irresistible urgency. I left the station, and to my great joy ran into a drugstore on top of the stairs. I rushed in and made my humble application to the man behind the counter. The sound of my voice must have moved him, for without any ado he stretched forth his hand and took a beautifully wrapped package from the shelf. 'AT YOUR NEXT DRUGSTORE,' I had been promised, and since this part of the whole promise had come through there was no doubt that the rest would, too. While I was waiting for the next train, which took considerable time, I sucked some of the lozenges and took a few more during the short ride. The effect was telling. The moment I found myself again in the street my throat was perfectly clear.

C   Congratulations to you and also to myself. For I am now going to enjoy my first talk with a brand new Tester.

T   You seem to have forgotten the point of my whole story.

C   I am glad there is a point.

T Didn't I tell you before that something made me think of you?

C That I have really forgotten. When did those friendly thoughts materialise?

T When I found myself completely cured and yet, and yet . . .

C Did you suffer a relapse on your walk to my place?

T Not at all. The disappointment was much deeper. For though I felt like a new-born babe so far as my throat was concerned . . .

C Were you crying then?

T Don't haggle over phrases. I am going to stick to the one I used. My throat was new-born, but I myself was the old Tester and so I am still.

C Bad for me, too. You must have felt deceived.

T The lozenges did me really good. It was rather the glorious implications of that strong promise that caused its literal fulfilment to be followed by a severe shock.

C What had you expected to happen?

T I had been hoping that after my obeying the message of redemption time itself would come to a stand-still. A full enjoyment without change or hindrances. A complete transformation to make me as light as a bird. Nothing behind me but beautiful memories, nothing before me but ever more lovely prospects. A happiness ever dreamed of but never yet realised. Now as you see me—nothing of that kind has come through.

C Did you buy enough of that precious stuff?

T Enough and to spare. Share some of them, for they are really good.

C Share what? Reality or myth?

T Those words of yours or some others to the same effect I anticipated when I tried to search into my shock. Therefore I thought of you and our last talk.

C You mean that part of it that dealt with idols?

T Especially your remark that your analysis did not cover the whole range of idolatry. During the week I tried to make it up but somewhat stopped half-way. To my surprise that ridiculous experience I told you in so many words pushed me much further.

C Now in these lozenges I want to have a full share.

T   You are welcome though what I have to offer is not palatable.

C   Why not?   The last time we talked about nasty idols, but now it seems that you have come across the attractive ones, those with the beautiful promises.

T   The fulfilment of which throws you into an abyss of despair. But let me start from our last talk as I have tried to digest it. The idols with which we dealt one might call idols of justification. For they served us to vindicate our self-worship before the tribunal of our conscience.   When we posed as ardent patriots who pour their rage over their political opponents it was not a true love for our country that inspired us.   Our real motive was of a possessive nature.   *My* country, emphasis on the possessive pronoun.   By being abused as an idol our country is made the munificent contributory of our enlarged self.   I am no longer that poor creature I used to know.   I am myself *plus* my idolised country.   That is what all too many people mean today when they call themselves proudly Americans, British, Frenchmen and so on.   Having drawn my country into my larger self, I feel great, noble, admirable, worthy of all the worship my pride and self-righteousness have been rendering to my ego ever since.   Thus I try to invalidate the protest my conscience levels at my deep-seated lust of self-deification.   The other class of idols to which I now turn one might call idols of deliverance.

C   Deliverance from what?

T   Think again of my lozenges.

C   No, thank you.   My throat is in perfect order.

T   I asked you to *think*.   'Redemptive'—what a tremendous ground for hope.   All will be well with me—if I only take Redemptive.   All, I said.   If it were only a sore throat—that might, of course, cause expectations of relief, but the promise contains more, far more, exceedingly more.   I am still understating.   It is a difference in kind.   The evil of which I shall be ridded is no less than my full personal share in the pathetic plight of suffering humanity.   Though there is a relation between it and my throat pains.   It is a symbolic or better a representative relation.   Even a trifle of a cold may stand for that whole realm of earthly misery from which the producer of Redemptive pledges to save his customer.   Other competing offers work with different representatives of the same evil, but that makes no noteworthy difference.   There is always a more or less discreet innuendo to the effect that unless something is done soon you are going to sink into the bottomless pit. This intimidation proves a very effective preparation for the great announcement of salvation to follow. You don't suppose I have only the mythology of advertisement in my mind.

C   I don't. Some of its managers are great specialists in innuendos, which leads me to ask whether that whole branch of business is not sort of secularised revivalist preaching, at least of the more recent type. As to the technique employed the difference seems not all too great. I think, however, that idols do not always draw by force of intimidation. The really dangerous ones don't.

T   True, but even here a strong reference to our creaturely misery is made, not explicitly, of course. It is rather inherent in the aggressive Gospel as proclaimed by the many and different idols of deliverance.

C   How would you define an idol of deliverance?

T   I would call it the mythically enhanced object of any desire or passion. The object may in itself be a good or a bad thing: it is always the enhancement that makes it an idol. At the same time, it makes our desires run wild, defying control. And as I said, this is never affected by the mere content of the promised object. It is done by the promise as setting itself against a background of sheer gloom. The offered remedy implies the diagnosis of the illness. That is why every idol promises redemption.

C   From a sense of guilt?

T   That is always there and sometimes furnishes the peculiar material with which the false promise works. Yet in every case the frame of reference is much wider. The mere appearance of that beautiful image, the appeal it makes to sensuality or to personal aspirations and ambitions, to a longing for security, to a thirst for rest and peace evokes by contrast a reaction of self-pity. It brings into focus our heaviness of body and soul, our loneliness, exposure, frailty, frustration. And behind these and similar feelings is the pressure of time itself, the unrelenting necessity of surrendering all you have and are.

C   'The groaning and travailing of the whole creation.'

T   Yes—'and here,' says your idol, 'is where I come in. Accept me as the dominating power in your life and I shall rescue you from all your pains and ills.'

C You let the idol speak. Since idols are dumb, who is the ventriloquist?

T The idolator himself and what possesses him. The whole uncanny attraction the idol exercises on me is only the charge with which I have loaded it. My idol can promise me no more than what I am promising myself. For in the ultimate issue I presume to be both the redeemed and the redeemer.

C If that is so what then is the function of our idols? Why do we prostrate ourselves before them?

T We even prostitute ourselves to them. That is the right word, for it indicates that the whole affair is only a bargain. Idol-worship is no worship at all. It knows of no submission or surrender. In clinging desperately to my idol, I do not respect it. I rather annex it. I may be absorbed in its embrace up to my extinction. That is just a trick to make the idol part of myself. The magical or mythical power I draw from it shall serve me to strengthen my presumption that I am not a mortal but rather a god. With this presumption strengthened I can flatter myself to lord it over myself. This fundamental lie constitutes the negative response to the challenge of the human situation—but always under the guise of meeting its true nature.

C So our second class of idol-worship has turned out to be self-worship no less than the first.

T There is one practical application I want to draw immediately.

C There are many, very very many.

T Unfortunately you are right. And there is no real precedence. I feel, however, that we two are bound to make good what we missed a week ago.

C No doubt about that. When you said before that you had been thinking of me I expected some criticism. Since then, I have been waiting for it.

T Not yet, not yet. Our discussion started with politics and we never lost sight of it. When we said goodbye we were perhaps too tired to draw the political conclusions explicitly. Shouldn't we do that now?

C No doubt we should.

T I knew that was on your mind, too. For neither you nor I are bothered by the Chinese puzzle whether theology should

serve politics or politics serve theology. Let all things work together for good, and there will be no more sham problems.

    C We have enough real problems. What were *your* political
        conclusions?

    T Our discussion led us to see through some of our unholy
        passions. If we act on what we learned, if we enter the fight,
if we remain engaged in it, destroying our own idols with the help
of God, as often as they emerge under whatever guise—then we
shall be better equipped for fighting idolatry in public life. Think
of the many cheap remedies we are offered, daily, as, for instance,
the iron broom man who promises to spare us perennial vigilance
by wiping out corruption once and for all. Again think of the
current ideologies that should be better called idologies. Look at
those enchanting pictures of permanent national health or of
definitely established social justice: 'This picture I painted with my
heart blood (or, for that matter as the result of invincible scientific
method), will turn into glorious reality if you give me the necessary
power to deal with the devil and his hosts. Vote for me, support
me, fight with me, and my power will be your power. My picture
on every wall symbolises your own divinity, to be established under
my leadership.' The moment a political opinion turns idolatrous
its contents no longer matter. There is no essential difference
between a murderous utopia and a deadly restoration of a past
that never existed. I do not, of course, limit idolatry to ideology.
The self-glorification of racial, religious or historical groups is so
extremely spiritless and dull that it does not even bother with
ideological justification. It simply steals its justification from its
hate of other, 'inferior', groups. Let's no longer talk about our
minority problems. Let's rather be frightened at the terrific cauca-
sian and all the other majority problems. Here as everywhere it is
not enough just to call evil, evil. It is not even enough to stand up
against it—so long as the true nature of the evil remains hidden
behind a superficial diagnosis. The respective statements may be
correct but they must lack vigour—so long as we are looking only
in the direction of psychological, sociological or historical 'causes'.

    C Nor are we furthered by mere moralising or general religious
        exhortations. Let's be specific. Whatever splits a nation in
an unnatural and perilous way goes back to the self-worship of
individuals and groups. If every one is to himself a god—no wonder if the result is a clash of gods. And mind you, those gods are

pitiless, much less amenable to human feelings than the crudest savage. If we would but start attacking every one himself we might one day discover a better procedure for dealing with our political differences. But how can we attack ourselves seriously, how can we give up idolatry without worshipping God with our mind, words and actions?

T Here is the hub on which everything turns. In realising that and sticking to it we can laugh the reproach of quietism in the face. We shall simply ask our respective critics who is likely to be better equipped for action, a drunk man or a sober one. One might even accept the label of quietism considering that quiet heart-searching leads to improvement, while noise leads to nothing but greater noise.

C All that refers likewise to our international relations. There are and always will be political tensions between nations. What makes them so dangerous and costly is the clash of the gods. I know from myself and from much I saw that nationalist self-glorification is far deeper-seated than most people dream, including those who honestly oppose nationalism in principle. If we would be better aware of this inner danger we might learn to approach some of our baffling international problems with a healing sense of humour, so far at least as this side of the iron curtain is concerned.

T Could you illustrate your point?

C Cheerful clamour versus unintelligible understatement; crude self-indulgence versus hallowed tradition of stage-acting; urging a responsibility to be taken by others at great risks versus refusal to take sufficient responsibility at not so great risks; naive but self-conscious engineering versus complacent insistence on how complicated things are; quick reaction without consideration versus slow consideration without much action; fatherlessness versus paternalism; Mercury's benevolence without energy and skill versus Mars' energy and skill without any benevolence; denouncing nationalism at home, while encouraging it abroad versus fostering it at home and denouncing it abroad; unceasing protestations of friendliness versus increasing suspicion of protestations; real generosity versus fear of ulterior motives; sacrifices promoted by a bad conscience versus robust threats in order to wring as much as possible from a bad conscience; self-assured invectives against colonial exploitation versus exploitation without imperialistic interference; realism mixed with military expediency versus idealism mixed with profitable neutrality. Well that may do for the time being though, of course, the list is far from being complete.

T What about communist Russia and her satellites? Here humour will not bring us very far.

C I did not pretend that humour alone could help us. Its contribution is one of mellowing in the course of which many an acerbity is removed. Humour is a great reconciler, but if we go on serving our idols no sense of humour can save us. We can never dispense with humour which is integral of true humanity, but we can avail ourselves of its healing power only if our worship of God becomes more real. Then we shall not only talk politics but, above all, pray politics. Otherwise neither God is real to us nor are politics. I know, of course, that many people will smile at that. They look at prayer as an excuse for inactivity. They don't know better. Therefore I am afraid that much of their present boisterous activism will end in frustration and defeatism. For what can we do without the help of God. Let us never relax in calling on him, thanking him for what we have been spared and asking him to grant to all nations peace, freedom, social and economic justice. Our prayers will be answered, first of all, by our own receiving a little bit more wisdom as to the right balance between necessary military preparedness and an energetic peace-offensive that lacks the smack of propaganda. We shall also better understand that we can neither rule the rest of the world nor can we withdraw from it like an offended ballerina. God rules, he alone, and we have got to obey him in our inner life as individuals, as groups, as a nation and no less in all our relations to the other nations. God answers prayers. If only a few people would take prayer more seriously, and taking it seriously entails the responsible recognition of the fact that prayer obligates him who offers it—if we would really pray politics, who knows? God may spare us the horrors of another World conflagration by removing its causes.

[*Silence. Then Tester speaks*]

T Let us start with it now.

[*Period of silent prayer*]

T I don't feel like continuing our talk today.

C So I shall have to wait until next week for your criticism.

T If any of it will be left by then.

PART III   An Inverted Conversation

Same persons, same place.   One week after the last talk.

C   Today, you cannot accuse me of keeping comfortably at home, while you are taking troubles.   Though I draw little satisfaction from it.   I feel rather sorry at that boiler business in your house.

T   Don't worry.   The thing will soon be in good order, and the trip to your home was all smooth and uneventful this time. No story, no thoughts . . .

C   Except your critical postscript to our discussion two weeks ago.   As I told you over the 'phone I am all ear.

T   Shall I start with a summary of our talk before last?

C   That's a good plan.

T   All right, then.   When we had listened in to the news we were both hot with anger.   I accused you and your political friends of having settled in a cloud-cuckoo-land where the only reminders of reality consisted in the daily unearthed corruption affairs.   You did not, of course, back up corruption, but just because you couldn't you retorted with a fierce denunciation of McSmearism.   Since I couldn't back up McSmearism, I concentrated on those issues where I felt stronger.   You gave me tit for tat and so we paddled on, though we felt both that we were paddling against the current.   Suddenly you came out with the suggestion to stop criticising God.   I felt much surprised and didn't understand you at all, but then you convinced me that our anger was mainly a tactical device to get over the shock we had suffered from the revelation of our political jumble.   There was a higher purpose behind our being shocked.   We should be brought to realise that we are only people.   For we had claimed, at the bottom of our hearts, to be more than people.   The events that make us feel ashamed were Divinely calculated to shake our pride and reduce us to our true human stature.   We, however, had persisted in our pride.   We refused to accept the wholesome Divine judgment, and in a twisted reaction against the chastisement we had received, treated our respective political enemies as his Divine majesty's whipping boys.   I asked you why we had reacted in that twisted way.   That led us to an analysis of conscience or rather the particular manner in which man argues with his conscience.   We know that we cannot exist without establishing ourselves before the tribunal of conscience. It is for that reason that we cover all our wrong thoughts and doings with a rosy varnish. Either a man obeys his conscience or he rationalises his motives. There is no third term given, since we can never part with our conscience. The fact that we have a conscience and must constantly try coming to terms with it, demonstrates the omnipotence of our Creator who has established his fifth columnist in the centre of our own being. Whenever we try to cheat him by cheating our conscience, we are only cheating ourselves. That must not be taken in a narrow and trivial moralistic interpretation. Behind all our moral failures stands the original sin of self-worship. The many and different idols we set up in our hearts shall only serve us to justify our basic self-deification against the protest of conscience. We have but one chance as individuals and as nations, to do the truth by shattering our idols and worship God instead of ourselves. Do you accept this as a fair summary so far?

C   It is a fair and good summary. Just go ahead.

T   Up to this point I have no criticism to offer but am only grateful for the instruction I received from you. Don't be silly and protest now, you did instruct me and that very effectively. As to my doubts—they all concentrate on your notions or let me frankly call it your particular doctrine of the Divine-human relationship. Let me try to sum up your principal assertions. We meet God constantly in daily experience as he addresses us through every life situation. The language he uses in addressing us are the facts and events, great or small, that constitute the situation. Through them he calls us to worship him in acts of the spirit that embody themselves in our words and deeds. We, however, have strayed too far from his presence in order to understand his language. Our dull hearts are closed to it. The Biblical Revelation makes his voice audible to us by strengthening our conscience. Thus fortified, our conscience brings his message home to us. We then react either by making a true response or by running away, covering our flight with so many excuses. If I understand you right this is your system of references to which the whole drama of human life is related. And here is exactly the point where I doubt that I can see eye to eye with you. My attitude is not merely negative. There is enough common ground to make continuation of our talk imperative. In fact, I didn't wait for our meeting today in order to resume it. During the last couple of weeks I have kept on talking to you in my mind and listening to your possible replies.

C   I hope the debate did not grow all too hot.

T   Let me record the main points.   My first objection drew its force, as it seemed to me, from our common basic assumption.   I better call it a resolution.   For quite early in our talk we made up our mind not to engage in theoretical investigation of what happens on the ground of the soul or elsewhere.   We would rather think and speak as people who are working on themselves.   Was not that the fundamental understanding at the bottom of our whole discussion?

C   It certainly was.

T   Thought must issue in action.   I wondered, however, that your statements concerning God and man could be expressed in terms of action.   Were they not rather attempts at solving metaphysical problems?   Suppose you did offer the right solution—what follows from that?   When I asked myself this question, the result was a certain feeling of emptiness.

C   Sort of the-morning-after-feeling?

T   Not quite though perhaps something similar.   I was looking in vain for a goal where the many thoughts we had developed could lead us.   Then, after some time, I knew or believed to know what you would have said to that.

C   Show me the child you have begotten on my behalf.   I hope I shall not have to disown it.

T   'Is the worship of God not an action?', you asked me.

C   Recognised.

T   You also pointed to practical consequences, for instance, the political ones we had drawn a week ago.

C   They were rightly drawn, but I would never use them apologetically.   But what was your reaction?

T   I agreed only with regard to the undisputed part of your statements.   That the worship of God is an action, the one, indeed, that should carry all our actions—I did not for a moment deny.   I maintained, however, that your reply was too vague and general.   I challenged your ideas of immediacy, sort of relationship where I am the one partner in a continuous dialogue and God is just the other.   Is that doctrine equivalent to an effective call to worship?   I felt on the contrary that it suggested an intimacy with God that made me sometimes shudder.   I am not going to introduce the ambiguous term, mysticism.   For what on earth has not

been called mysticism?   Some people use it merely as a frightening
bogy, others, quite differently, as a pass-word for joining some
faithless pack of irresponsible literati.   Others again who are good
Christians but bad Protestants have given the word a more or less
legalistic connotation.   Some of them indulge in a saint-worship
which I consider wrong with Roman Catholics and physically dis-
gusting with others.   Since you have nothing in common with any
of those abuses I shall avoid the term as I tried in my mental
arguing with you.

    C   Did you have to try hard?   Or did you hear me laugh at the
           reproach of mysticism?

    T   I admitted that if God manifested himself through a given
           situation and not beside it, the term mysticism would be mis-
applied in its possible connotations.

    C   So you did not attack me from that corner.

    T   I attacked you from the impregnable fortress of Holy Scrip-
           ture.   'God is in heaven, and thou art upon earth.'   We
know of no other Divine Revelation than is contained in the Scriptures.   Nor do we need any other.   The moment we leave this firm
ground our feet are liable to slip.   It is true, you did not use the
word revelation in this connection.   You used manifestation or
took to a philological vocabulary.   'God addresses us,' you said,
'he speaks to us.'   I found that rather ambiguous.   'In this whole
sphere,' I said, 'we are encountered not by the actual Word of God
itself but rather by our own thoughts.   Even if those thoughts are
sometimes challenging, well, a man may challenge himself yet
without pretending that it is God who challenges him.'

    C   Did I reply to your objection?

    T   Oh yes, you did.   First, you said, it was not scriptural at all.
           In order to prove that you quoted from Amos, Deutero
Isaiah, the Psalms, the words of Jesus and the first chapter of Paul's
letter to the Romans.   I rejoined that your interpretation of those
places was literalistic, taking little account of their moral connection and intent.   You accused me of diluting the Scriptures by
reducing their message to not much more than mere ethics.   When
I protested that you must have entirely misunderstood me you
hurled some invectives against theories of value-judgment.   I en-
treated you to let the dead bury their own dead.   You insisted that
my viewpoint must lead to impoverishment, leaving us hungry and
thirsty and what not.   I doubted that and warned you of theologi-

cal sentimentality. Driven by despair, you mounted the big guns. You declared rather rudely that my negations made the whole Scripture Revelation pointless. Either it referred us to the will of God as confronting us here and now or else it bore no reference to anything at all. It was rather I, you added with sarcasm, who intellectualised the issues.

C I feel not impoverished at all but only enriched for having been lent your temper. I regret that I was not present to witness the mood in which you made your definite retort.

T For some time I had none to make. Unfortunately, I gave myself to wicked thoughts, regretting that I had left several of your assertions uncriticised two weeks ago. When I saw that this was neither fair nor to the point I pulled myself together and hit you back. 'I don't deny,' I said, 'that the teaching of the Bible points us to our actual experience. What I must deny is your forced and overstrained interpretation of our experience, especially the part you assign to God.' I took you by your own words. 'What does it really mean,' I asked. 'What can it only mean to say that the will of God is manifest here and now? It means that we have to obey him by loving him and our neighbour, here and now. That does not in the least imply that actual facts and events are the terms God uses in literally conceived conversations with us. There is no need for introducing airy conversational concepts. So long as you are using metaphors as metaphors and keep conscious about it I raise no objection. Unfortunately, your position is a more ambitious one. It smacks of a programme. And this I must repudiate. Let us feed on bread and not on candy. Faith, obedience, love bring us into a close enough relation with God. The rest is metaphysics,' I concluded.

C Was that the end of the discussion?

T Oh no. You didn't give in. On the contrary, you were rather rough with me.

C I regret that. It is not nice for a man to play a rough part in his friend's thoughts. Give me the chance to detest my roughness.

T Or rather to enjoy it. What you did was accusing me of deism. My conception of God, you said, made him hardly less remote than the God of Descartes of whom Pascal remarked that his main business consisted in rapping the World on the nose in the beginning, then leaving it alone.

C Pascal was right but I was wrong. For how could I have attributed a position to you which you certainly disclaim?

T Do you think I cannot see through your malicious irony? Just wait a little. The story is not finished yet.

C Now I am getting really afraid.

T Quite reasonably. For as I was not prepared to pocket that affront I took offensive steps immediately.

C Which was the only possible thing to do.

T 'There can be no doubt,' I said, 'that we are immediately related to God. He holds us in his hands every moment. Yet that does not place us on the same conversational level with him. It does not permit us, no, that is still too weak, it positively prohibits us from telling a story about what is going on between him and us.' When I had made this point, I felt that I was moving on safe ground again. I remembered having made it on several occasions, first during our talk before last, then also in my many debates with your ghost, but somewhat it had come to nothing. I might have lost it in the heat of the battle. This time, I resolved to stick to it and never let loose again. 'You called me a deist,' I exclaimed, 'for the only reason that I am pleading for some more reverence. What has the one to do with the other? I insist on nothing but a greater awareness of who God is and who you and I are.'

C That looks far more the real Tester than all the rest of your arguments. I heard you once say that none of us was brought up along with God on the same school-bench.

T Is that not true?

C It is perfectly true and very timely. I have often felt reminded of it in these days when nearly every sweet Sunday school girl feels deeply convinced that God could not do for a moment without her gracious assistance. That may be nice with Sunday school girls though I would never teach it to them. It is horrible with adults and most horrible when proclaimed from the pulpit. I guess it must have been hard for me to meet your attack.

T I don't know. True, you looked stunned for a few minutes. Then, however, you lifted your arm and dealt me a heavy blow.

C Not I. What did you suppose me to have committed?

T You said that a due sense of reverence for our Creator and supreme Ruler must never be used as a pretext for arguing his presence away.

C What was your reaction?

T It was quite contrary to what you desired. Just because your counter criticism made me feel unhappy I got pretty obstinate. 'Suppose,' I said, 'you hit me now, that does not improve your own position.'

C Did you leave it at that?

T Not for a long time. After I had recovered, I made you some concessions.

C Good for me.

T That remains to be seen. My purpose was to make my own position unassailable in order to attack you more effectively.

C Aren't you a tough fighter? The next war bulletin please.

T I would no longer deny your assertion that there was something like a story of Divine action and human reaction. 'Yet,' I added with firm conviction, 'while we are playing our true part in that story, we are in no position to talk about it. The moment we talk about it, we do not play our part any longer. We are given to sort of spiritual loitering. Then, one soon feels tickled by certain interests which stir him to produce lots of problems and their solutions. One may fill a whole life-time with this business. And that sails under the flag of theology! Now what do you say to that, Claimant?

C What did I say to it?

T I asked you because I didn't wish to make you responsible for the arrogant aphorisms your ghost shot at me.

C In order to honestly regret his impertinence I should have to know what he said.

T Lots of things I disliked. I don't remember all, but I kept what I resented most. You pretended that the pathos of my charges against you was Kantian rather than Christian. I knew from my own reaction that you had touched a vulnerable spot. I could not blame you for that, but the way you put it was simply not nice. I made you feel that, whereupon you apologised.

C Which spares me apologising now.

T Don't irritate me again, for this present remark of yours proves that I was unfortunately successful in conjuring up your ghost. But let me finish my report. Your apology put me in a more reconciliatory mood.   You may smile at it now but what you said soon afterwards induced me also to offer an apology.

C   The end of your report promises to be its most interesting part.

T   Sorry if I have bored you until now.

C   Not at all.   I ask you to pardon me if my remark . . .

T   [*laughing*] We are, it seems, both in an apologetic mood. Isn't it silly to feel like apologising for having been frank and free from inhibitions?

C   Well, as we discovered the other day, we are no more than people.   What was my ghost's last utterance?   His swan-song before giving up his ghost?

T   You asked me with some emphasis whether I could really prove you guilty of *telling* a story of Divine-human relations. Then I felt at once that I had no right to accuse you of loitering. For who knows?   What I called telling the story might be part of your personal assignment in the story.   You had to do that just in order to act your proper part.   What about my part then?   My criticism of you exhibited now some cocksureness of which I did feel sorry.   At the same time, I found it difficult to assess to what extent I had been wrong.   Also my misgivings about what I called —perhaps maliciously—your system of references have not entirely subsided.   And here I am, sometimes in a combative mood, at other times nearer to contrition, but on the whole rather perplexed. Can you do something for me?

C   I feel like trying to stir up your opposition.

T   Impersonating your ghost?   That is a noble offer.   For it implies inciting me against yourself.

C   I cannot help that.   For we must come to know where each of us really stands . . . Let me take up the debate on story-telling.   I must, indeed, endorse my ghost's protestations.   I believe that the story of God's dialogue with every human-being will be told, once, on the day of judgment.   Then it will be made plain in a way that makes denial absolutely impossible.   For the telling of it will be identical with its definitive interpretation, fact interpreting fact.   *We* can interpret facts only by thoughts.   I never undertook to offer more than thoughts.

T   I have to admit that.   The whole question turns on what you understand for thoughts.   What are the objects of your thoughts?   There is, on the one hand, God, speaking to us through

people, things and events. There is the word of God in Scripture
that impresses itself on our conscience. There is our conscience
that point us to the actual Divine message. On the other side of
the picture are we with our self-worship, our idols, our excuses.
The forces thus being arraigned, the battle can begin. Now in
focusing my mind on this picture I must ask myself what I am
doing. Am I going to review the work of God? What is my title
to embark on such an enterprise? If I try nevertheless, what is
my motive? Setting my thoughts over against the reality I mean
to grasp? Enjoying my grasping it? Comparing my mental
picture with the reality it reflects and drawing satisfaction from the
similarity of the two? 'Here it is. Got it.' In many cases that
might give you an innocent pleasure, but not here. For here God
is part of the reality I subject to my search. I say I subject it.
Can God ever be made subject to us, be it only mentally? Can we
approach him in any other way except by humble faith?

    C We know God before we believe in him. That knowledge
        does not at all mean lording it over him.

    T Suppose you are right, can we ever produce the knowledge of
        God? Can it be made the aim of our investigation? Is it
not rather given to us quite independently of and rather in opposi-
sion to our conscious efforts? Are not those efforts suspect as
such? To me, at least, they seem to be.

    C It depends on from where our thoughts start and where they
        lead. If they arise from what you called loitering, you are
right in questioning them. If they arise out of an unescapable inner
necessity you may be wrong. Again if they lead out of the human
situation into those empty plots where some people of genius have
built their magnificent systems, you are right. If they lead deeper
into the situation of man as being claimed by his Maker, then you
are wrong. To think means to prepare. It means to admit with
Socrates that you are not where you ought to be, then turn in the
right direction. As you put it: to work on oneself. Whenever
we two face this task we are on common ground. I am not conscious of leaving our common ground if I ask you now why it is
that your criticism was not aimed at and, indeed, did not bear on
the substance of any of my statements. There was not a single
assertion to the effect of things being not so but otherwise. The
real aim of your criticism was the way I might have misunderstood
my own statements. What I said I might have understood right

the moment I said it but slid back perhaps only a moment later. 'No one who puts his hand to the plough and looks back is fit for the kingdom of God.'

    T   It is true that I joined issue not with what you said but with the meaning of what you said. Should I have failed to do justice to your intentions, my criticism would quickly recoil on myself.

    C   Certainly not before having done a good job somewhere else.

    For I am by no means above your criticism. I see no reason for retracting ought of my statements. My own attitude to them, however, is in a constant need of revision.

    T   Then I should, at least, have given you the benefit of doubt. Though . . . that is perhaps not the proper way of putting it.

    C   You should have attacked *me*, leaving my statements alone.

    Not that I would place my statements in heaven. Yet I believe that the primary function of criticism is to help one's fellow to recover the true meaning of his own utterances.

    T   Don't you sacrifice yourself for the sake of your children?

    C   The contrary is true. I am looking for my personal advantage.

    T   If that is so I feel encouraged to look for my advantage, too. So please don't take my restrictions but hit me back sharp.

    C   I don't know whether I can. [*Slowly and determinedly*] It seems to me that the danger of *your* theological position . . .

    T   [*interrupting*] Do I hold a position there? I am trying hard to extricate you and me from any so-called position.

    C   That reminds me of a talk we had long time ago. 'Let everything else explode,' you exclaimed then, 'and Christ alone remain.'

    T   I am glad you did not accuse me of nihilism then nor are you going to do it now. You may, of course, object that my attack on standpoint-theology reflects just another standpoint. Be this as it may, if you wish to attribute a standpoint to me, it is, at least, not an academical one.

    C   A fact on which you sometimes seem to congratulate yourself.

    T   Now you have at last started doing me good. Just go ahead.

    C   If somebody should complain that your particular position or by whatever name you call it, makes all further discussion impossible you would, of course, rejoin . . .

T That in this case we should have to carry on without conducting discussions of the kind Mr. Somebody takes so seriously.

C To which I raise no objections. The question is, however, whether your present statement like the one I quoted a moment ago is not exposed to the same type of misunderstanding to which any statement is exposed. It may even lend itself easily to ambiguity.

T If that is so, and I have no right to doubt it, then I shall have to . . .

C Extricate yourself from just another position.

T I don't intend running away. State your case against extrication.

C In order to illustrate it I shall quote from what a very great man and writer once said in extricating himself from any theological interest in the doctrine of the Atonement. Quote: We draw a veil over the sufferings of Christ simply because we revere them so deeply. Unquote.

T [*passionately*] Who was the man?

C Tell me first what your reaction is.

T I don't believe him a word.

C The stuff was written by the German poet Goethe.

T I should have guessed at Goethe. Nobody else could have put such a beautiful garment around a naked lie.

C I got the quotation from a famous and epoch making history of Christian dogma. The author supplies Goethe's excuse with his warm personal approval.

T Scholarship is not proof against folly, not even the scholarship of a genius is.

C Both cases illustrate the danger of a certain theological detachment, and if you forgive me this remark, it is not just a matter of temperament to be on your guard against . . .

T Lack of real concern. [*Interval of silence*] 'Thou art the man.' Now you have really done me good, Claimant.

C I do not at all deny that it looks ridiculous and really is, to put a new find on the market of contemporary thought. It somewhere hurts your sense of shame. You must have felt like this in recalling some aspects of our discussion.

T I don't know. What I know is that I am fed up with my objections.

C That does not settle anything. What we both need and in
an equal measure is reaffirming our common resolution as to
the nature of theological thought.

T That is, indeed, the central issue now.

C There are thoughts and thoughts. The ones that can now
only come into consideration are the actual movements of
the spirit in opening itself and making itself ready to meet him,
who is already there and has ever been. His presence is clouded
to us because of our unreadiness. We have shut ourselves in. Go
and open the windows, one by one. That is what I understand for
theology.

T If you opened the windows yesterday open them again today.
Otherwise you are in danger of confusing your mere recol-
lection of yesterday's window-opening with the fact itself. To
change the picture: A sign-post points you in the direction you
ought to take in walking. If you don't walk but only gaze in the
indicated direction you have missed the message of the sign-post.
Then you may start wondering what the whole sign-post should be
good for. Also your memory of the services it once did for you
becomes dull and confused. The-morning-after feeling you mentioned before. Here is the reason for all my doubts and objections.

C Which were very helpful, indeed. Or do you think I don't
need being told to march forward instead of collecting
treasures that crumble to dust in my hands?

T I am sure, we must continue our talk on God's fifth columnist.
After all that has been said we can do it only by making a
fresh start. It is too late for that now. Can I have your promise
to come to my home a week from today?

C God willing, I shall be there.

PART IV The Storm

*Same persons. The scene is at Tester's home, one week after last
talk.*

T I am glad you are looking well. That's the only piece of
news for which I didn't inquire on the telephone. There
should be news of another kind though. I am asking myself how
to start proper inquiries.

C   Let me suggest it to you.   A highly respected friend of ours, when I saw him the other day asked me straight away how my theology was.

T   That makes a very good question, first because it reminds me of our friend, second because I can adopt it wholeheartedly now.   Well, Claimant, how do you do?

C   Troubles, troubles.

T   What caused you troubles?

C   The memory of our last talk.

T   That causes me some apprehension.   I know your good memory can be vindictive.

C   It does not withhold from you what is your due of appreciation.

T   I like you to enlarge on this subject, though still with apprehensions.

C   You did a splendid job of traffic policing.   I received several tickets for parking in a prohibited area.   On the highway, you insisted from time to time that I was running into red lights. I tried a detour, but you called me back, shouting that this was a one-way street.   Finally, when I was at my wits' end not far from complete despair you surprised me by giving me a green light.

T   You see.

C   It was already too late for getting anywhere.   That's enough for one day, I thought.   Since then, I have resolved that on the next occasion you should take the driver's seat.

T   What do you want to make of me?   Am I your driver or a member of the force of which we are all so proud?

C   No offence.   Have one of my cigarettes.   It's a new brand.

T   Thank you . . . err . . . It's too late to refuse now, but for the future I must advise you that the department has been thoroughly reorganised.   Nothing can deflect me from the path of stern duty.   You pay your traffic violation fines or else . . .

C   Pay to whom?   To the police?   I wonder at the efficiency of departmental reconstruction.

T   You are wrong, sir.   I want to see the receipts only.

C   I have none to show you.

T   You have none at all.   And that man dares to cast suspicion on the department.   I am going to show you . . .

C   Since you have succeeded in convincing me of your unimpeachable integrity, I am quite ready to make a full apology.

T   An apology that is given so condescendingly means nothing
but another abuse.   You better leave me alone with your
arrogant pleas.

C   I am really sorry.

T   Rightly so.   Don't think that finishes the matter.

C   I would like to see the matter honourably arranged.

T   What was that?   Trying it again with dark allusions?   You
don't know me yet.

C   I really didn't mean . . .

T   I see what sort of fellow you are.   You have the audacity to
deny a man his sense of honour only because you know the
man is terribly underpaid.

C   You are referring to being underpaid.

T   Not to arouse your pity . . . Or . . . what do you really . . . ?
I am not going to put up with your impertinent distortions.
Either you stop talking or I'll arrest you on the spot.

C   That's easier said than done.

T   I have your licence number.   I'll see to it that the next time
you . . .

C   You will never see me drive a car.   Here is my car, here is
my key.   Do with it whatever you will.

T   Have you gone mad?

C   May be.   Of course, if you like the proposal we may both
get into the car and you drive me straight to the next good
restaurant.

T   You dare me?

C   Don't interrupt before I have finished.   We shall both have
a substantial dinner there and you will pay the whole score.

T   I have no more time left to spend with a mad man.

C   Just because I am a bit deranged I need the protection of the
police.   On the ground of your own evidence my present
mental state does not permit me to drive a car . . . Don't you see,
Tester, that I can stand my ground?

T   You are driving me mad.

C   I don't want to drive at all.   That's the whole point I want
to make.

T   [*laughing*]   Now tell me, why don't you . . . really . . . ?
Let's give up this comedy.

C   I am quite serious about continuing it though not exactly on
the same line.

T What is your purpose?

C Cross-checking.

T Playfully?

C That depends. I believe we shall both have to go on the stage, each acting the other's part. That's, at least, my suggestion.

T It is a twofold suggestion. Tell me first about cross-checking.

C A week ago, you concentrated on what in a more serious sense than is usually attached to the word might be called the method. Before we parted, we decided to continue our talk on God's fifth columnist. We understood that we should have to make a fresh start in order to proceed farther. That requires our recovering the ground of our first discussion on the subject. We cannot make deductions from accepted premises. That would be quite contrary to the method we clarified a week ago. At that time, I wondered about your challenging my approach yet leaving the substance of some of my assertions uncriticised. Where do you stand now? It would be silly of me to expect a dry thesis in reply. No, let us face the same reality again, but in a way that compels each of us to understand the other while keeping his own eyes open. What I am looking for is agreement, again not a ready to be put in the pocket agreement, but one that results from each of us seeing what the other sees. For this reason I suggested impersonating one another. The procedure is unusual, but I hope it may lead us to a clear decision on up to what point you can follow me and I can follow you. It is, of course, an experiment.

T Well, I have nothing to lose after what happened last week.

When you first mentioned cross-checking, I was astonished as I thought of laboratory procedures or statistics or so. That was, of course, foolish.

C Just in order to avoid the mere resemblance of test-tube methods I want us to act. Moreover, this arrangement has merits of its own. Let me state it this way. We two fellows are to face the same reality, each from the other's angle. You will state what you can see under your adopted point of view. I shall have to challenge your statements from your former presuppositions which I shall honestly try to make my own. The result will be that each of us is compelled to give account of whether or not he is in a position to share his fellow's premises.

T Who will feel unhappier during the performance, you when you see me bungle your position or I when you will caricature my negations? Nevertheless, let us take the risk. For the result is worth its while, if it can be attained.

C I am hopeful. The reality with which we have to do *is* one and the same for both. And we take one another seriously enough in order to try to sit where the other sits. In some measure, we did it already in our previous mental dialogues yet my present suggestion offers the advantage of a real talk. Still, I believe that our many discussions with one another's ghost (for I did as much of this kind as you did) might have prepared us for our present business. There are, of course, many temptations to stray.

T What shall we do if we get into a muddle?

C We shall have to try getting out of it again.

T All right. Before we start we must, of course, agree on where to start. I have thought of this during the week.

C I am glad you did. I rather concentrated on matters of procedure.

T The motor that kept our first talk on the subject going was your initial warning to stop criticising God. Could we not be met with the same reminder in a different setting so as to check on the way the reminder must be interpreted?

C That would be very helpful, indeed. The question is only how to get the proper setting. Or can we ever produce a situation? We must rather take it as we find ourselves placed in it.

T There are situations in which we find ourselves every day. We neither produce nor invent them. And the simpler, the more commonplace they are, the better for our purpose. For if your main presupposition is right, then, what happens between God and us must also happen while we are dressing or shaving, walking, shopping and so on.

C There is no point in dressing or shaving just now. Nor is there any shopping on Sunday. Would you like going out for a walk?

T On a day like this? It is far too cold for that. Besides it would be a rather ridiculous way of seeking to produce a situation.

C [*laughing*] Did you take my words seriously?

T Only for a moment.   There is not much imagination required
     in order to cover a walk [*pointing to the window*] through
these empty plots that stretch . . .

C Northward, I guess.   It's rather airy over there.

T That meets the case. So let me try. After leaving the
     house, you feel, at first, strengthened and refreshed.

C Very much refreshed.

T By the resistance your body offers to the grim cold.   Yet the
     storm is blowing and the bitter frost gets the better of your
nose, your ears, your chin.   It stings, it pains: You are looking for
some temporary shelter.   There is no shelter.   What will happen
with us?   I guess, the first thing each of us will do is asking himself
who it was that made the stupid suggestion to leave the house on
such a cold and windy day.

C Looking for the whipping boy?

T Right.   I must correct my narrative.   The thing we did
     already previous to asking the questions of fact and guilt was
giving room to a certain resentment that rose in us, slowly.

C Perhaps not quite so slowly.

T A resentment which implied much more than the mere reac-
     tion to physical discomfort.

C I might feel tempted to calling the weather names.

T As we are all doing throughout summer and winter.   Fall is
     fine, and there is hardly any spring.   More recently, however,
I started feeling embarrassed by that business.   The other day,
when the snow was melting into a grisly sauce, I called the weather
lousy.   Well, I don't know why it was just on this occasion that
something in me protested and rather strongly.   I knew I ought not
to do that, and the reason was not merely aesthetics or manners.
You understand me . . .

C I do.

T We are now in a similar situation.   Calling the weather
     names yet feeling uneasy about it.   Now let me ask you.
Who is the weather to be called names?   And why do we feel so
uneasy about this popular reaction?

C You cannot kill two birds with one stone.   Let me first
     answer your first question.   The weather in general and the
present storm in particular are by all means mere physical events.
Can you honestly contradict that?

T Don't pin me down to a sterile alternative. Things are not as simple as that. Mind you, the way one reacts against those mere physical events is rather remarkable. You feel shocked at being laid open to a vicious attack. It ought not to be so. There should be some method of engineering the weather. Unfortunately, there is none. The respective gadget has not been invented yet. But that's wrong. The elements ought to be at your disposal instead of somebody else's. For there is somebody else at the background. Though you protest against him you do not dare to face him. There is something in you which prevents that. So you will inculpate the weather or yourself who suggested this outing or me who was foolish enough to consent.

C Well roared, lion. By now I can see where the result of your self-examination will lead you. Quite obviously, you indulge in personifying the storm. Well, that happens, sort of recurrent animism. I hope it does not indicate some neurotic disturbance. For that might cost you lots of money.

T Not me, since I have nothing to spend on treatment.

C That may be good for you. Leaving the question of diagnosis aside, one thing we shall have to admit. The fact that you are reacting personally does not prove that you are reacting against a real person. Conclusions of that kind would be utterly fallacious. I hope you are not going to claim objective validity for a mere projection of your subjective feelings.

T Well shone, moon.

C Thank you for calling me names.

T Excuse me.

C It is all right.

T Truly, the moon shines with a good grace.

C Begging of your Grace to add a few words of commentary to your very kind appraisal of my poor production.

T Your supplication is granted. My comment is that you ran very fast. By now you are a good deal in advance of me. Did you ask me whether the direction you took is the one I intended to walk?

C I just warned you from going in a wrong direction.

T Your warning presupposed that I was about to explain a known effect from an unknown cause. Is that the procedure to be used in our discussion? As one of us stated some time ago, we are dealing with matters of conscience.

C   That is just what I wanted to point you to.

T   I don't know.   You pretended that we were looking for a
causal explanation, then warned me of using a wrong sort of
causal explanation.   You should know that this sort of approach
does not come into consideration in our present discussion.

C   I am sorry for overdoing my part.

T   You should not have made this remark.

C   I know, but I hate being unfair to you.

T   Leave this to my care please.   Even foul play I would prefer
to acting out of character.

C   I am all contrition.   Please go on where I interrupted you.

T   You made a very appropriate remark a few minutes ago.
When I said that a certain resentment rose in us, slowly, you
doubted that it came so slowly.   Were you serious about that?

C   I am always serious.

T   Except just now.   Serious or not, your remark reminded me
of the shock character of our reaction.   Let me try to work
that out.   A shock always comes suddenly.   Not that what caused
it needs to be a sudden event.   The storm which offended us may
have been blowing a long time before we left the house.   Nevertheless, the moment we reacted we felt like being stabbed in the back.
What happened to us was entirely unexpected.

C   How could it have been unexpected?   That you will feel
uncomfortable, being in the open on a day like this, is the
most natural thing in the world to expect.   There is very little
imagination required in order to anticipate it.

T   I have not made my point strong enough.   What we resented,
intensely, was not one of the many unexpected events that
may cause us an unpleasant surprise.   It was the unexpectable as
such.

C   [*speaking aside*]   He is doing well.   [*aloud*]   In my modest
opinion, a questionable statement does not gain in convincing
power by being expressed in stronger terms.   Strong or weak, you
better make it plain to me.

T   I say, the suddenness was not in the event as such.   It was
characteristic of our realising the meaning of the event.

C   You refer to the moment when the cold started to tell on us.

T   Not necessarily.   Our reaction might have set in a bit later.

C   Delayed action?   We wanted to be patient but had to give up when our pains grew worse, or when our supply of hand-kerchiefs was exhausted.

T Nothing of that kind would account for the specific nature of our resentment. Something else had to happen before.

C Are you going to introduce a new factor?

T No new one. We mentioned it already before.

C I don't know what you mean. Solve this puzzle for me, please.

T It was not before our conscience struck that we unleashed our pretentious indignation.

C You did introduce a new factor. For in our story so far as I can figure it out, our conscience rebuked us only after we had called the weather lousy. You are antedating its intervention.

T The one to which you referred is already the second in our story. I am dealing with the first now.

C Which means enlarging the story, I hope not by legendary accretions.

T You will check on that. What I am going to do is telling the story more accurately than before. Pain as such does not humiliate a man. *Yet humiliated we were, and that was what we resented.* That was also what came so suddenly. At one moment, our presumptions of being something great and big were given the lie.

C When should that have happened?

T Some time after our growing feelings of discomfort had passed the threshold of consciousness. Before that, our con-science could not have struck.

C Whether it rebuffed us or not, seems to me immaterial. That our pains grew more intense, must be attributed to the storm. That intense pains evoke additional feelings of indignation, is a simple psychological phenomenon. You make far too much of all that.

T We cannot, of course, predict whether our conscience will strike in a given situation or not. We don't lord it over our conscience. But one thing is certain. The moment conscience really strikes no psychological mechanism can account for the lesson it administers to us. In our present case this lesson is one of humiliation. The indignation you mentioned presupposes humiliation, that is conscience has really interfered.

C There are feelings of guilt, some of them of a rather complicated nature, which have been ably described and at length
discussed during the last decades. It is not correct to undercut
proper investigation by making conscience the common denomina-
tor of many different reactions. There are clusters of problems
that cannot be that simplified. After all, it is not in the interest of
conscience to use it as a pretext for re-establishing an all too primitive psychology.

T I for one have a very good conscience about not dealing in
this connection with our sense of guilt, not thematically at
least. I believe that the modest claim of truth must have precedence over the claims of a proud profundity.

C My respect for your personal feelings does not dispense me
from asking for an explanation.

T The question that clinches the issue is whether in the situation described we are occupied with our own feelings of guilt
or rather with the storm. If the first is the case we do not follow
the lead given us by our conscience. If for the sake of illustration
conscience may be personified I should say that it does not take
pleasure in accusing us of our guilt. It throws us back on ourselves, but it does not leave matters at that. It calls us not to
introversion but to action. It leads us inside only that we might
find our way out of ourselves and meet what we ought to meet,
there.

C That brings us back to the storm.

T True. Tell me now: Could a mere physical event as you
called the storm have humiliated us?

C In a way it could. We were shown our weakness and frailty.

T That is no reason for feeling humiliated. One may be a very
big human, morally speaking, yet frail in body and sensitive
to the inclemency of the elements. A storm may crush you but it
does not lower your moral stature. In our case, however, we were
brought low from a state of presumption.

C Well, people sometimes do presume. I have no interest in
a dogmatic denial of your statement. I can even admit that
our conscience raises its voice against our presumptions, on many
occasions. Why not also in your narrative? I can feel quite com-
fortable in admitting all that. One thing, however, gives me to
think, and that is the context in which you place the protest of

conscience and the meaning you attach to it.   Tell me, Tester, did you ever write from your conscience's dictation?

    T   What do you mean by your question?

    C   When we speak of the dictates of conscience, do we take it literally or metaphorically?

    T   Metaphorically, of course.   The dictates of conscience do not consist of words.   Conscience does not speak.   It just points.

    C   Right.   What was therefore the function of conscience in our story?   When we came to realise that we were suffering from the cold our conscience did not introduce any new material.   It brought no further content to our experience.   It just moralised it. Our realisation of a resistance that showed us our feebleness was interpreted as a deserved punishment or personal defeat or whatever you call it.   Do you agree, or do you think it was different?

    T   I agree.   Our experience was one of moral refutation.

    C   Which means that our conscience in some mysterious way supplied a moral interpretation of a physical sensation. Then, however, and considering your claim for the unconditional precedence of truth, we cannot be forbidden to ask whether this interpretation was true to the facts or not.   Honestly speaking, that is honestly pleading on your behalf . . .

    T   Aren't you cutting a poor figure, Claimant?   Pull yourself together, man, and act your part decently.

    C   I beg your pardon.   Sticking to . . . excuse me.   Let me boldly ask you whether the treatment our conscience gave us was a fair one.   As for me, I doubt it.   And that is my answer to your second question concerning the nature of our embarrassment. We called the weather lousy, perhaps with good reason.   Our conscience blamed us for that.   Perhaps it was wrong.

    T   I wonder whether your questions and doubts are so bold. In my opinion, only plagiarised.

    C   I don't claim originality.   Whom should I have plagiarised?

    T   Yourself and me.   For when we called the weather lousy, we did exactly what you are doing now.   We argued with our conscience.

    C   Suppose for the sake of argument we did it really, then we did in a twisted manner what I am doing honestly now.

    T   Provided only it is possible to argue with one's conscience honestly.

C You are defying conscience. That makes just another kind of self-worship. Or are you not aware of that difference there is between God and our conscience?

T I hope I am. Are you for your part aware of the difference between defying conscience on the one hand, and realising that it testifies to God, on the other?

C Be this as it may, in its actual interpretation of a given event conscience can be definitely wrong. There are errors and there are sicknesses of conscience, some of them widespread. You must also know that conscience has had its history and a rather long and complicated one   Shall I tell you some stories?

T No, thank you. I was brought up on that.

C So you must know better . . .

T What I know is that physiological, psychological, sociological and historical conditions can make for a widening or a narrowing of the range within which conscience operates. Then, there are the general human vices of ignorance, prejudice, superstition. They exercise a tremendous influence toward narrowing the range. Nevertheless, within the sphere to which conscience is reduced it still works. Its voice may be muffled and almost stifled, but you cannot extinguish it altogether. When you expect it last it returns with new vigour. As to the errors and sicknesses of conscience, I think we already dealt with some important aspects of them.

C Where and when?

T When we discussed false ultimates. Something wrong is done in the name of right. Whenever that happens we act decidedly against our conscience but always under the pretext of heeding its appeal. For that is the only way we can run from it. To ascribe our various subterfuges to conscience itself is equivalent to charge our debts to our creditor's account. It is the old subterfuge, only in a theoretical form. We may speak of sicknesses of conscience, but then we do it in a similar way we refer to nervous sicknesses. To call a neurosis a nervous sickness does not mean to ascribe its cause to an irritation of nervous tissue. Correspondingly, what we call a sickness of conscience is in fact a sickness of the mind that perverts not our conscience but our understanding of its mandate. Concluding, let me state that relativism with all its modern scientific trappings is only a sort of escapism. It leads us out of our true situation which is lit up by the flashes our con-

science issues.   Therefore, if you want to make a point, be specific.
Take the concrete situation of our story, then show me that and
why our conscience was wrong.

    C   It was wrong in offering or suggesting a moral interpretation
        of physical events.   I challenge the validity of that particular
kind of logic.   And that is my point.   I am up against the confusion of two quite different spheres, the ethical and the natural.
What about distinction of categories, boy?

    T   Also on this I was brought up as I may acknowledge with a
        far greater sense of gratitude.   I was not, however, taught
that distinguishing between the two realms means tearing them
asunder.

    C   They are interrelated in the purpose of our Creator.

    T   In accordance with which and as an echo of his voice our
        conscience did its interpreting.

    C   The burden of the proof is on you.   I have formulated my
        objection.

    T   That the mere distinction of categories does not lead us all
        the way through can be shown from a study of the book of
Job.   Job complains about his terrible sufferings and gives proof
of his courage and godliness by bringing his complaints before God.
His arguing with God he does not do on his own behalf only.   He
turns advocate for all suffering humanity.   Finally, God answers
him and proves him wrong.   Job acknowledges the Divine correction.   He humbles himself, repents in sack and ashes.   He confesses that the Divine answer has brought him a fresh knowledge of
God in comparison to which all he knew before was mere hearsay.
Now tell me exactly what the Divine answer was that clinched the
whole issue.

    C   You point to the most difficult problem that the book of Job
        poses.   For there is no positive Divine answer.   There are
questions, one after another, very pungent questions, but none of
them seems to permit of any answer except the negative one that
Job cannot understand the mysterious ways of God.

    T   The questions to which you referred are asked in connection
        with what you would call poetical or at some places perhaps
mythical descriptions of?

    C   Well . . . the Leviathan, the Behemoth.

    T   And . . . ?

    C   What did you expect me to call them?

T Going on strike? No rest for the wicked. Whether I was right or wrong in my anticipations, you speak up your mind.

C My own mind?

T Mind your part, Claimant. How often must I admonish you?

C I am sorry, but it is a sense of shame that interferes.

T You should temper it with some sense of charitableness in order not to expose your brother's reasons for being ashamed.

C It would be most uncharitable, indeed, to ask you on whose behalf you are pleading now.

T I don't know what is worse, your lack of discipline or your mental cruelty.

C You really misunderstood me. My sense of shame was not vicarious but quite genuine. I stuck to my part more seriously than you thought. There was no intention of being cruel. And if there could be any reason for ever being cruel, you certainly did not offer it to me.

T I am not quite sure how to take your words. It does not matter. Let me tell you plainly what reply you would have to make from your point of view.

C It is mine no longer. I am going to give up.

T In that case I could not take your place. For it would be too much to attribute to me, the real Tester . . .

C Who is the real Tester? All your former gracious admonitions have now found their way back to yourself.

T I am really sorry. To make amends I will now supply what neither you nor I would have seriously maintained.

C Who is you and who is I? And who is serious about his part? I don't know what kind of checking can be achieved if each of us shows his real feelings . . . Pardon me. I shouldn't have made this remark. It only contributes to our confusion. You see I am in a muddle. Aren't you, too?

T One of us said before that if we found ourselves in a muddle . . .

C We should have to try getting out of it.

T That is, at least, a fact about which we cannot be muddled up.

C Thank you. You have made me more co-operative. Let me state, then, that one who wished to oppose your arguments at any price would call the earth and the sea, morning and dawn, light and darkness, snow and shower, the stars in the sky, the beasts of the field, even the gate of death . . .

T I won't be so cruel as to let you finish the statement. Natural phenomena. Or rather physical events. That was the word used.

C Thank you, especially for your courtesy in omitting the attribute, mere.

T I only forgot it. Since you have recovered your courage I am due to recover our argument.

C Yours please. I am at my post again.

T Splendid. Now all those humiliating rhetorical questions which bring out Job's ignorance I take for interpretations by the author, of the one thing God really does in encountering Job's plea. And that event is a very simple one, do you remember?

C Isn't that remarkable? I never thought of it until now. And when I say I, I mean I, the real . . . err

T Your sins are forgiven, but go and sin no more. [*speaking aside*] It is, indeed, remarkable, for also to my mind it came only this moment. [*aloud*] Go ahead, my friend.

C 'The Lord answered Job out of a storm.' And we were talking about an outing during a storm.

T My preliminary conclusion is that according to the book of Job the interpretation our conscience gives of the message of a storm might after all be justifiable.

C I don't say anything now. It all depends on how you will work it out.

T Let us concentrate on what convinced Job of being in the wrong. His final act of penance proves that he was conscious not of an error but rather of a wrong moral attitude toward God. I think that is established beyond doubt.

C Job was made to feel that his criticism of God had been irreverent.

T He was made to feel it in virtue of an actual Divine reply. This is very important. Job repented not for having infringed upon a general ethical principal to the effect that one must never argue with God. Such a principle was maintained by Job's friends in their hackneyed attempts to plead the cause of a God known only by hearsay. Job, however, needed an actual Divine message to become frightened at his rebellion against a God who dealt with him and taught him, here and now.

C   True. It was not a conventional God of pious memorial verses but a living person that revealed himself to Job.

T   By speaking to him out of the storm. Let us now ask more accurately what it was that brought about the change in Job's attitude.

C   That's just what puzzles me. God did no more than letting a storm blow, adding a few peals of thunder. What is the convincing power of those events?

T   The first thing we can state is that they showed Job his ignorance. He who can do what God does knows what he is doing. Job does not know. Why not?

C   Because he cannot thunder.

T   That brings us nearer to the centre of the argument. The meaning and purpose of things and events are only perspicuous to him who made them. Since Job is not the Creator he has no right to question the actions of the Creator. That includes even his own misery. Just because Job is innocent of his misery he has no title to challenge the rule of him who ultimately caused it, thus must have known why he caused it.

C   That's rather radical. Still it keeps within the book's theological horizon.

T   Which is certainly no narrow horizon. Now to our problem. The maker and ruler of the universe gives in his works shattering proof of his unchallengeable knowledge and power. But does that also prove that his works are good, morally speaking? They perfectly serve his purpose, though that purpose might be an entirely heartless one. Like an engineer's constructing a perfect and wonderful machine, but whether he does it for good or ill, who can tell?

C   Again I admit that your questions are within the book's system of reference. For Job in his complaints did not challenge the knowledge and power of God. He challenged his goodness. He accused him of cruelty.

T   There are two ways of dealing with our problem. The one is just giving up. One may state then that the greatness of the book of Job consists in posing and elaborating a tremendous problem rather than in offering a definite solution. The other way is trying to understand the change in Job's attitude and the reason for it. I leave it to you which way to choose.

C   Don't ask silly questions but go ahead.

T Then I must say that that change must have been mediated by Job's conscience. It was the interpretation given by the man's conscience to—let me cautiously state—not merely physical events—that made him bow before his maker in sack and ashes.

C Maybe or maybe not. I can only repeat that you are due to work it out.

T You suggested before that such interpretation may be arbitrary. Suppose, however, this one was not arbitrary. Or would you call it unmethodical to give Job's conscience the benefit of doubt? I believe not doing it must be called unfair.

C You are kidding me. If I had known before what burden I would have to shoulder, I would have never suggested it.

T Don't get sentimental, I hope you will soon be given back to yourself.

C This time you are unfair to your part. But I am no better. Let us keep some more discipline for the rest of our round.

T Agreed. Now if we are gracious enough to give Job's and, for that matter, our own conscience some benefit of doubt we have to look for a possibly valid starting point for its work of interpretation. There may be some foundation on which it builds. Where shall we look for such a foundation?

C With the storm.

T So let us ask whether or not there is something in a storm or about a storm that lends itself not to a projection of our feelings but to an adequate appreciation of what we have until now expressed in negative terms only.

C [*speaking aside*] He is on the right track. [*aloud*] What did we express in negative terms?

T We denied that the storm was just a natural event. Since you shared in this denial you may perhaps state the reason. I make this suggestion not because I am lazy but in order to increase the accuracy of our cross-checking.

C Don't deceive me. You are pitying me.

T Or for that matter myself.

C Your self-pity is contagious. Woe me. First I must negate your assertions and now I have got to negate my own negations. Are you sure that a negated negation will make a position? We are not practising mathematics. Besides, your suggestion makes me feel giddy.

T Never mind feeling giddy.

C I submit. Some minutes ago, when I named again some of the beings and events described in the last chapters of the book of Job, I was again impressed by the beauty and majesty of the description. I believe that an authentic poetical description does not represent a mere projection of our feelings into the things described. It does in its own way justice to what is in the things. They stand for more, far more than the most accurate and exhaustive analysis given in scientific prose could ever express. If we mean by natural events such as come under the supreme competence of natural science so that nothing essential could be said about them after science had spoken, then, I must confess that that use of the word, natural, deprives us of a whole dimension of truth. Or to put it in another way. If the physical characteristics of things and events exhaust their being, the counter-claim must be raised that things are more than they are.

T They are always more than objects. Does that affect our conscience?

C It does. That is, if we do not turn away by making the depth of reality the object of a mere aesthetic pleasure. Such pleasure is offered us as a springboard. To keep standing on a springboard and gaze around is silly and ridiculous. Sometimes, it is wicked.

T If I understand you right you imply that the sphere within which conscience operates is not limited to what one calls the ethical.

C That depends on what you understand for the ethical. To restrict the authority of conscience to a man's obligations towards his fellow or to himself—that I would call a miserable falsification of facts.

T I am very interested. Could you specify your assertion with regard to our present subject? How is conscience related to the revelation of beauty and majesty?

C It claims our respect for what touches the soul. It teaches us reverence not only for life but for the background of grandeur and delicacy which is, virtually, everywhere.

T You have made a strong case, Claimant. Let me continue now.

C I have not finished yet.

T [*laughing*] You seem to enjoy the reversal of your part. In fact, Claimant, I believe it is time, not to reverse our positions, for that is no longer necessary, but just to work together.

C [*smiles*] What about our cross-checking then?

T I have a confession to make. While you were speaking just now I became aware of the fact that many of my former doubts and objections were due to that narrowing of the concept of conscience which you called a miserable falsification. There is a sort of pseudo-ethical idolatry which, in blatant contrast to what it intends to achieve, leads to the result of deafening our ears to the voice of conscience. It has a stunting effect. I feel very happy at the prospect of being delivered from that vicious prejudice.

C It is widely spread today.

T I know. [*moment of silence during which the storm is heard*]
It is left to me to acknowledge that my doubts and objections have come to nought. It is true that God speaks to us through the actual situation. I must say that I ought to have better listened to ... your ... [*A tremendous blast. A door is banged in the vicinity*]

C [*after a period of silence*] Let us in all reverence follow this lead. Does this storm really account for its own awfulness? Does it not rather with its whole being point beyond itself?

T It does. Its power expresses a powerfulness that posits and carries it.

C This is what must have convinced or rather convicted Job.
When the united manifestation of the powerful and the awful confronted him he knew that he had spoken irreverently. For at that moment he knew that he was spoken to, personally. *And that he was spoken to* he understood as an undeniable manifestation of the goodness of God. The God who spoke to him cared for him. The power that communicates itself to my inward being is the power of supreme goodness. It respects me as a spiritual being. It imparts itself to me in its manifestation. It meets me, person to person. As it imparts itself to me in its message I know that I am his own.

T No storm, taken as an abstract physical event could have brought that meeting about. It was God who came to Job out of the storm.

C It falls to me now to state explicitly that the message of the book of Job does settle the problem of a moral interpretation of so-called natural events. There is one more question to raise in this connection.   But aren't you too tired for continuing our talk?

T   Let us finish our job.

C   So far and not even so far as any job can be finished down here.   Do you believe that we, today, are exactly in the same position as Job?

T   We have just experienced the book's message coming to us with the force of a contemporary event.

C   That is true, yet there is a difference.   Job in his previous life was never what we call an atheist nor can we suppose him to have met atheists.   We, on the other hand, live in a society where there are atheists and some of them rather vocal.

T   What follows from that?   I do not think that an atheist should be treated differently from anybody else.   Any special considerations of his case would only flatter him by taking his arguments—if he has any—more seriously than they deserve.

C   I did not refer to arguing with atheists.   I am not fond of fuss either.   One must consider an atheist and treat him as a man who is in the presence of God—like the rest of us.   But that was not what I was going to say.   I believe that the difference between Job's and our historical situation is that the presence of atheists or, for that matter agnostics, in the midst of us compels us to elaborate and pursue our theological questions with the greatest possible radicalism.   Not only that we owe it to them— and we do owe it to them—but, first of all, for our own sake we must accept the challenge of theological nihilism.   Its mere exist- ence places us under responsibility to gain our own insights *vis-à-vis de rien.*   The knowledge of God we attest must be a fresh on the spot gained knowledge.   Otherwise, it was never anything but stale. Taking the difference of conditions into account I can say with you that we are essentially in the position to which Job remained true when he refused to join in the trite protestations of piety by his friends.   There is, of course, no necessity for you or me to act the part of an atheist now.   We did already enough acting, and what matters more, I perfectly agree to your refusal of giving atheists special treatment.   Only that we must take them, and that means in the ultimate issue, God who lets them be with us, more seriously.

T   What is your suggestion, then?

C   Going farther in the same direction we have pursued till now.

T   All right.

C We need more clarity about what conscience does in interpreting our actual situation to us.

T I am very interested. For a while I wondered whether the
term, interpretation, was altogether fortunate.

C I think I can defend its use. Our conscience is we ourselves,
therefore interprets. For everything that is active in us, even
on the lower levels of our nature, interprets. What is colour but
our sensual interpretation of the same reality which physics interprets as light waves? When the reality we symbolise as light waves
of a certain length exercises its influence on our retina, we see the
colour red. The wave itself is not red, yet when we see red we do
not falsify reality. Our eyes give us a picture which is not only
useful and beautiful but expresses in a specific character what
hits the retina. That picture does not show a wave of light. It
shows something quite different, a colour. It is not a mere re-
duplication of what it represents. It is its interpretation. The
same with taste. When we sense the sweet of a grape we interpret
what physics describes as certain molecular interactions. Those
are unknown to the lay-man, but for that matter the interpretation
of the underlying reality by our tongue and brain does not do less
justice to its specific character. And so on. In certain cases of
sickness or minor functional disturbances our sensorium gives
wrong interpretations. The exceptions prove the rule that what
we experience in a normal condition is not imaginary but real. It
is subjective, but that does not make it untrue. It is creative on the
basis of given facts Our sensorial interpretations of reality are
true to the facts as they concern us. What they represent are not
the bare facts of scientific analysis but, nevertheless, real facts in
their interrelation with our body. When it tastes sweet, we say
that *it is* sweet. There is no contradiction between those two statements. The grape *is so* that to our tongue it offers a sweet taste.
At the same time, *we are so* that on the fundament of the grape's
melting in our mouth we can and must build an interpretation
which consists in the sensation of sweet. Our tongues and nerve
centres, etc., teach us something about the true quality of a grape.
Of course, very many other qualities remain neglected in our interpretation, but as far as it goes it is true to its object. Different in
kind as it is from the reality it represents it nevertheless. It corre-
sponds to it. Now that was perhaps the longest discourse I delivered

during our whole talk. I am afraid, it is going to be continued with your permission.

T I beg you to go on.

C Under the same point of view we may now consider our conscience's interpretation of a storm. There are many important and really interesting things to tell about a storm—of which our conscience does not take notice. It limits itself to what concerns us here. The concern now in question is not of our body or mind but . . .

T Our concern as moral beings, as persons.

C Accordingly there is an immense difference in kind between this interpretation and the ones we considered before.

T This interpretation is unique in its being authoritative. It makes us responsible.

C Thus showing us what we are. For I believe that the most important aspect under which the difference between man and animal can be viewed is our responsibility as established by our conscience. Being responsible, that points to the very substance of man.

T I can agree since I have now been brought to realise that responsibility is not a narrow, moralistic concept confined within the boundary of mere obligation.

C We must all give up that legalistic idea of conscience.

T The moment we get rid of it we arrive at a richer and—I dare say—more joyous understanding of responsibility.

C It is rather inclusive. And that makes a man feel happier.

T Like having broken out of prison. It feels like inhaling good fresh air.

C We said before that our conscience does not introduce new material to our mind. It does not increase our knowledge, that is its quantity. Yet it teaches. What does it teach us?

T Responsibility.

C Here much depends on what we understand for responsibility. Would you say that accountability is in the centre of the concept?

T It is rather a corollary, though a necessary one. When I think of responsibility in the present connection I rather take it literally: We are called to respond . . . The call to which we must respond is made with an absolute authority. It vindicates its perfect legitimacy in a manner we cannot challenge. Whatever issues, the call is right far beyond any possible doubt. That is proved, indirectly, by the impossibility to disobey the call without offering excuses. We can never meet it with a straight and honest No. For it establishes itself with a force of undeniable conviction.

    C You have put it clearly, and the only contribution I can add to your statements is negative. I trust that when this negation is considered the *positive meaning and scope of responsibility will reveal itself without any of our doings.*

    T What is your negation?

    C Conscience never points to itself. The overwhelming authority with which it has been invested, its irrefutable power of conviction is never pushed in the centre. Whenever that is done, it's not our conscience that does it. It issues its call; it dictates, but it does not claim our response as to be offered to itself. Conscience does not lead us out of our true situation. It can never be made an object. It does not seek its own. It is in us; it is we ourselves; it never pretends to be our *vis-à-vis.* It does not aspire to exist for its own sake. It drives us out of ourselves to meet our real *vis-à-vis.*

    T It would then be improper to say that we are responsible to our conscience?

    C We are made responsible by it but not toward it. The servant knows and testifies that he is not the master. Whoever takes the servant for the master, disregards both the servant and his master. He who worships his conscience by relating our responsibility to it and stopping there, simply worships himself. I cannot prevent a man from doing that. I can only tell him what he is doing. If he is not a perfect fool he will not like me telling him that.

    T [*after interval during which the storm is heard*] It is, indeed, a most vicious thing that we miserable, self-centred beings fancy to be self-centred what is destined to deliver us from the grip of self-centredness. And yet, the temptation is great and always close at hand.

    C Which proves how clever the tempter is and how busy. I agree with you. To say that we are responsible to our conscience, to our conscience alone, suggests itself like the most self-evident of all assertions. It sounds so serious. It comes so smoothly. It grasps us so easily. Just that should serve us a warning. For it takes our pride unawares. Let us take up our thread.   To whom are we responsible? . . . What was that? [*walks to the window*]   Some tiles from that pile over there.

T	Thank God, there is no need of treating our question in a general and abstract manner. Our conscience never does that. It works in a concrete situation which it interprets.

C	And its interpretation consists . . .

T	In relating us as persons to the author and speaker of this storm.

C	No storm in the world could ever reach our conscience. God does it through the storm.

T	I think that people of old who believed in storm gods saw farther than many of our self-styled educators today. Though they were not clear enough about what they saw.

C	I do not want to trifle, least of all now, but there is one point in your statement I cannot accept as accurate.

T	What is it?

C	You should not have said that people of old believed in storm gods. The ancients would never have used that expression to describe their religious attitude. They rather said that they feared storm gods, that they worshipped them. Faith came later. It had to wait for the Covenants.

T	I admit that, but why do you emphasise it just now?

C	Because we are dealing with what precedes faith. We know God before we believe in him. We know him from his calling us. He calls us through his storm and our conscience.

T	To worship him. For that is for what we are responsible.

C	All the more since it is easier to understand for us, today, that it is not a storm god who claims our worship.

T	I agree. For our situation is dominated by the Biblical Revelation.

C	True, but in the interest of balance we should not leave science unmentioned. The meteorological explanation of the storm has made it clear beyond objection that it cannot have been engineered by a storm god. If we are looking for causes there are plenty and they are all natural. Behind the storm there is either nothing at all or the only God who made and sustains all things.

T	There are plenty of natural causes and that they are incomplete does not matter in principle. Suppose we had all the causes, even then and perhaps just then we should have to acknowledge that the fully explained causal nexus does not meet what we originally meant and still mean in looking for The Cause. For our category of causality is but a dim intellectual reflex of the quest of the heart in going out to meet the Creator—in response to his summons.

C   He summons our conscience out of the storm . . .
T   Manifesting his majesty.
C   And the futility of our self-worship.
T   And all our foolish claims.

[*Period of silent adoration*]

C   Now I feel rather inclined before I go to apply a tiny bit of psychology.
T   You?
C   With your leave. For it concerns you.
T   Woe me.
C   No reason for self-pity. Nobody is going to accuse you this time, not even yourself are.
T   That means quite a change.
C   You see, in trying hard to cut through one after another of our rationalisations, we sometimes fail to do justice to our better motives. I believe that at the bottom of your criticism a week ago there was not the extrication business or anything similar. You had more serious reasons for challenging our knowledge of God.
T   You mean the Biblical Revelation?
C   Not if considered as a formal instrument but rather in point of content. You must have doubted the wisdom of vindicating or trying to vindicate a knowledge of God which we have been betraying ever since. Because we have betrayed it we have lost it. Can we then reclaim it by means of talking together? True, we resolved to make our discussion an action or a series of actions. That still remains a one-sided affair. When God speaks to us out of this storm as he speaks to us through the convulsions that shake our country and the world at large—or even when he uses milder strains, should we not then be still and wait for him instead of presuming to interrupt his speech by our talking? True, our talking is intended to bring us nearer to a right attitude of response, to remove some obstacles at least. But is that not also a presumption? Who are we? Are we ever in a position to say to God: Wait a bit. I am going to try moving myself into thy presence? I wonder whether something like this was not at the background of

your mind?   Building a tower without calculating the means at our disposal.

T   That is true.   The whole affair seemed to me a bit too smooth.

C   If you had come out with that before . . .

T   I couldn't.   Though I tried it in a way.

C   I understand you very well from my own experience.   I was going to say that if you had formulated your scruples, for scruples they were rather than objections, then the reply I owed to you would have presupposed our whole present discussion.

T   Just for this reason I can now try making the reply myself.

[*after a while*]   If the response we owe to God is our worship of him, then we are never dispensed from entering the dialogue on the spot.   If there are obstacles we must try to get over them, for God wills that.   It is with the dialogue in which God engages us just as it is with the Divine Covenants.   The two partners are never on the same level.   If we take this to heart and stick to it—I have no more scruples in stating gratefully that our talk served the purpose of preparing us to take up the position assigned to us in our dialogue with God.

C   Thank you.   Have I to admit that our preparations are far from being complete?   The respective assertion is so ridiculously absurd that it carries even its denial into the same absurdity. Yet as you said, nothing dispenses us from making our response to God, be it no more intelligent than the crying of a babe.   And whatever help we can get we must bid welcome.   At the same time, I believe that our continued preparations must take your scruples into very responsible consideration.

T   Let us therefore understand ourselves in making a resolution to keep the horizon open.

C   That was also a fundamental demand at the bottom of all your scruples.

T   Thank you.

9. On the Problem of Time

i. The Flight of Time

(Psalm 90 and Eccles. 1: 1-13; 3: 1-15; Luke 13: 6-13)

ANOTHER YEAR IS GOING TO CLOSE. What was it like? Toilings and joy, blessings and visitations, expectations and frustrations, cheer and depression, experiences of great delivery and encounters with many petty things—and now it is all over. A year's time has been given to us, a year's time is being taken from us. How time flies!

The flight of time is a mysterious theme and also a very serious one. Let me just with a few words recall the age-old reflection on it as it issues from the very core of humanity: What is past—no longer exists. What lies in the future does not exist yet. Things past and future are not. Only the present moment is: Yet the present moment will be fleeing into the past and thus be brought to nought by the next following moment. Our real existence is like a tiny, frail island in the vast ocean of nothingness. Sooner or later the ocean will have devoured it. Our hour-glass will run down, there will be no more time left to us. *Memento mori*— be mindful of death—that is the message of every vanishing moment, the real meaning of the so often repeated, melancholic utterance: How time flies!

This in mind let us turn to our text, the Ninetieth Psalm.

'How time flies,' we said. Curiously enough, no such statement can be found in the Ninetieth Psalm, though it deals with the transitoriness of human life. Yet instead of stating that time flies, the Psalmist asserts that it is we that fly. For we read in v. 10: "We fly away".

Now this statement is not melancholic. It is rather serious. And just because it is serious it is not melancholic. If we say: 'How time flies!', we complain as if time and its flux were responsible for the vanity of human life. The Psalmist, however, seeks the responsibility elsewhere. It is not time, it is we, ourselves, that are responsible for our miserable plight. Therefore I said that the

Psalmist's statement was rather serious than melancholic. We are not the slaves of a blind destiny which fetters us with the bonds of decay. Nor is it the will of God, our Lord and Maker, that we should be carried along on the road to death, pushed from one fugitive moment to another. God still is what he has ever been: "our dwelling place in all generations". Whether we shall vanish away with every vanishing moment or find our rest in his eternal presence is left to us. Let us try to interpret the Ninetieth Psalm under this point of view.

"We fly away," the Psalmist said. Where do we fly? To death. "Thou turnest man to destruction; and sayest, Return ye children of men," that is to the dust of which we were taken. It is God himself who has made us subject to death and decay. Why? The following fourth verse begins with: "For". "For a thousand years in thy sight are but as yesterday when it is passed." That does not mean that the heavenly calendar runs somewhat slower than the terrestrial one. The message is far more personal. Supposedly you were asked just now: 'What happened yesterday?' and you would reply: 'Yesterday? Well, nothing of importance happened'. Suppose again you grew 1,000 years old and God would look down from heaven on the whole of your life, then state: 'These 1,000 years of human life are just as empty as yesterday when nearly nothing happened'. Or, as the Psalmist continues: "As a watch in the night". Think for instance of a soldier on night duty, guarding a magazine. What happened during the watching hours? Well, as some of you know, anything might have happened, but in most cases nothing happened actually. You were just bored, that was all. Now in God's sight 1,000 years of human history are as void and boring as an uneventful night watch. Why? God seeks our hearts, the only thing of interest to him. But where are our hearts? Hidden somewhere, far from his presence. We have withdrawn our hearts from God, we have betrayed him to what the futile moment offers.

But in vain. Hunting from one futile moment after another, we can never catch it. We are in advance of any satisfaction aspired for as far as our imagination is concerned. Yet we lag behind it in all our real experiences. We are running after phantoms only, like the thirsty wanderer in the desert who runs for a mirage. "All things are full of labour: man cannot utter it. The eye is not satisfied with seeing, nor the ear filled with hearing. Behold, all is

vanity and vexation of spirit" (Eccles. 1: 8). Our efforts remain
fruitless, meaningless. We worry ourselves to death, literally.
"Our years are like grass which groweth up. In the morning it
flourishes and groweth up"—it looks promising like our own youth
—"in the evening it is cut down and withereth". Yet while the
grass in the field just suffers its fate according to the law of nature,
our decay is due to our own guilt.

"For," the Psalmist starts again with "For" (v. 7) "we are consumed by thine anger, and by thy wrath are we troubled." Our
continuous defeats and frustrations are due to God's judicial action.
"Thou hast set our iniquities before thee, our hidden sins in the
light of thy countenance." We withdraw from God, God withdraws from us. His withdrawal, however, means death. "Our
years are carried away as with a flood." We spend them like a
mere thought, unexpressed in action. There is no real achieve-
ment, no substance, no true reality. It is all "as a sleep". For
when God withdraws his presence from us, all things withdraw
from us, too. Because we have fled from God, everything we long
for escapes us, moment for moment. Death is only the final con-
firmation of the futility of our existence, according of a divine
sentence of doom which is passed upon us, moment for moment.

Now I can explain the theological terms employed in this Psalm
as elsewhere in Scripture. God's withdrawal from us which frus-
trates, continuously, our selfish desires and expectations until the
light of our life is extinguished—Scripture calls the wrath of God.
Our flight from his presence Scripture calls sin. Ignoring proudly
our God and Maker, we set up our own self as the centre around
which everything must revolve. For to every present moment and
to what it offers the ego would say: 'Stop, that I may swallow you
up, make you my own, keep and enjoy you for ever!' Thus we
stretch forth our greedy hands, but only in order to snatch at a void.
The sinister flight of time is only the reflection in our minds of our
constant failure to attain any satisfaction in God's absence. Who
deserts him is deserted by everything.

If this is our plight—what shall we do? As we are, we are all
inclined to ignore the spiritual issues of sin and of God's wrath.
We ignored them in favour of our dreams and illusions and did
it for so long that ultimately we became ignorant of them. Verse
8 speaks of our hidden sins. Our real life, what happens actually
in our hearts from moment to moment is now hidden in the dark

of our illusions. We are run-aways from God, run-aways from truth, run-aways from reality. We refuse to face the facts of sin and judgment. This our Psalm expresses in stating that we lack the fear of God. "Who knoweth the power of thine anger and thy wrath as fear would require it" (v. 11). Fear of God, as the Psalmist understands it, is the state of mind of a man who faces reality and the mood of mind which grasps a man who takes reality to heart. Only because one is afraid of reality one is afraid of the fear of God.

The Psalmist, however, shows himself not afraid of it. "Lord thou hast been our dwelling-place in all generations." Stayed on the Divine promise, he firmly believes that there must be a possibility for him to return to God and to take shelter in his eternal presence. But as he cannot find this possibility within the sphere of his own selfish will, he cries to God to grant it to him. He asks for such a vision of the truth which could strengthen him to seek God earnestly. He prays: "To count our days—this teach us, that we may acquire wise hearts".

What this means emerges from verse 10 where the Psalmist actually counts his days: "The days of our years are threescore years and ten; and if by reason of strength they be fourscore years, yet is their strength labour and sorrow, for it is soon cut off and we fly away". To count one's day thus means to take their vanity to heart, to take the Divine judgment to heart, to face the real inner self and thus to rise from the bondage of self-deceit. A man who in answer to his prayer is taught by God to look at himself as God looks at him, becomes filled with a horror of sin and judgment which drives him deeper into prayer. He knows that he is doomed unless God for his mercy's sake grants him, the fool, a wise heart. So he implores God's mercy to give him a new heart. "Return, O Lord, how long? And let it repent thee concerning thy servants." To repent as referred to God means that God may do the contrary of what he was doing just now. God had withdrawn his presence: The Psalmist asks him to return. And just this cry of a sinner out of the depth indicates that he withdraws from God no longer but seeks his presence. If we, however, return to God, God returns to us. This radical change of both our attitude to God and his attitude to us is expressed in a single word which occurs twice in our Psalm in v. 13: "Let it repent thee concerning thy servants", and v. 16: "Let thy work appear unto thy servants". Consumed by the Lord's anger, terrified by his wrath, the sinner cries to him for his merciful return, and while thus crying is changed himself and made the Lord's servant. The Psalmist uses the plural servants, as he is praying not only on his own behalf but for all the Lord's servants, the whole Church of God. Strengthened in his heart, he goes on praying, confidently, asking for greater and greater things which are, however, all concluded in the one gift of restored Divine presence: "O satisfy us early with thy mercy: that we may rejoice and be glad all our days" (v. 14). Let our days which drooped under thy displeasure be filled with joy and gladness at thy mercy. He goes on: "Make us glad according to the days wherein thou hast afflicted us, and the years wherein we have seen evil" (v. 15). Grant us to recover all that was lost during the past years of sin and judgment.

The Psalmist asks God to grant his servants joy and happiness, the object of their joy being God himself in his glorious manifestations. "Let thy work appear unto thy servants, and thy glory unto their children. And let the beauty of the Lord our God be upon us" (vv. 16, 17a). By his gracious dealing with his servants in delivering them from all their troubles, the Lord may reveal to them his work of salvation, his redeeming glory, the beauty of his loving favour. Thus the futility of our deeds and aspirations will be turned into solidity, our misery into blessedness, our failures into accomplishments. The same man who counted his days and found them void can close his prayer in asking God, cheerfully, to set up and confirm the work of our hands. What? To establish the work of sinful man? It seems that the Psalmist was conscious of the boldness of his petition, for he repeats it: "And establish thou the work of our hands upon us: yea, the work of our hands establish thou it". What a great example of living faith! As I said in my sermon on Luther, a fortnight ago: Faith is the bridge over the gulf between God and the sinner. By faith the Psalmist and all who let him lead them in their prayers were delivered from the reign of decay and death in order to stay in the presence of the eternal God. For them eternity has entered time, life has swallowed up futility. Nothing can be taken from them whose abode is not the fugitive moment but the eternal God, our dwelling-place in all generations.

Our Psalm offers no direct teaching on redemption, yet its message is one of redemption. For it proclaims faith in a God who can make his run-aways his servants, his outcasts his beloved children.   Thus understood, the message of the Ninetieth Psalm is prophetic and messianic.   It witnesses the mystery of the Old Testament saints' salvation.   Standing in the Divine promise, these men of God stretched out their faith through future centuries to touch the hem of the unknown Christ's garment.   "And as many as touched were made perfectly whole."

The Old Testament saints received, as it were, in advance of what should be wrought out in the fulness of time.   The fulness of time, that is the entering of eternity into time.   "And the Word was made flesh and dwelt among us."   In becoming man, the eternal Son of God was made subject to the condition of time, to the transitoriness of this world, to the curse of death.   He suffered it all and thus conquered it all, in virtue of his perfect self-denying Love.   Man in his selfishness is always the loser.   Love, however, does not lose anything as it never seeks its own.   When the Lord Jesus Christ lost his life for the sake of his love to us he kept it unto life eternal.   He rose from death and kept on living for us. He sent forth his Spirit in order to make us partakers of his love and joy.   If we follow him the flight of time loses its deadly sting. For whenever a man crucifies his selfish desires for the sake of Christ's love the miracle of Christ's resurrection is repeated in his heart.   Eternity conquers time, futility is overcome by the power of an irresistible life.   If we love God, if we seek in all things his presence nothing can be taken away from us.   Everything we have or may acquire is a Divine gift and every Divine gift is a token of Divine fellowship.   If we consider all that we have as tokens of Divine fellowship, then the token may pass away but that what it stands for, the Love of God, remains.   As Love does not covet anything, it owns all things in God.   There is no flight of time for those whose hearts are filled with Christ's Love.   Love is like a watch that keeps time, that is to say: it keeps up with what we call the flight of time.   Love never grows old.   For it is stayed upon and feeds upon the eternal God's victorious self-surrender in Jesus Christ.

So we need no longer complain that time flies.   The Old Year passes, a New Year is ushered in.   Let us greet the New Year, let us greet one another with what is not a mere wish, but an imperishable fact: "Jesus Christ, the same, yesterday, today, and for ever".   Amen.

"Nay, in all these things we are more than conquerors through him that loved us. For I am persuaded, that neither death, nor life, nor angels, nor principalities, nor powers, nor things present, nor things to come, nor height, nor depth, nor any other creature, shall be able to separate us from the love of God, which is in Christ Jesus our Lord" (Rom. 8: 37-39).

ii. The Time Allotted to Us

(Eccles. 7: 14 and 3: 1-17; James 4: 13-15; 5: 7-8)

MANY ancient writers, particularly among the Hebrews, wrote their books in the name of one of the famous men of the past. During the three centuries before Christ a number of books which have survived named as their authors Adam, Enoch, Abraham, Isaac, the twelve patriarchs, Moses, Elijah, Daniel, Ezra and many others. This was an innocent and often meaningful literary device that by no means involved something like forgery.

Some of those books were later incorporated into the Jewish Bible which is our Protestant Old Testament. A few more are in the Roman Catholic Bible while the majority are not recognised as sacred Scriptures though there are very good books among them.

Now among the ancients whom later writers impersonated the name used most frequently is that of King Solomon. For Solomon was famous for his wisdom and literary skill. Of the books that bear his name three are in the Bible, Song of Songs, Proverbs and Ecclesiastes. In the case of Ecclesiastes who actually wrote shortly before 250 B.C. the choice of the pseudonym is particularly fortunate and to the point.

The theme of the book is indicated by the initial and several times repeated exclamation: "Vanity of vanities! All is vanity". Later rabbis said poignantly that if an ill-tempered beggar had made this statement people would say, 'Of course, that's how he feels. What else could this poor, ignorant fellow have to say?'. It is quite different if you hear it from the mouth of a king who in wisdom, wealth and good fortune excelled all who were before him and came after him in Jerusalem. If Solomon is represented as calling life utterly futile one is rather inclined to listen.

Let us now listen to how Solomon applied his wisdom to the pursuit of happiness: "I made myself great works; I built houses and planted vineyards for myself. I made myself gardens and parks, and planted in them all kinds of fruit trees . . . I had also great possessions of herds and flocks, more than any who had been before me in Jerusalem. I also gathered for myself silver and gold and the treasure of kings and provinces; I got singers, both men and women, and many concubines, man's delight.

"So I became great and surpassed all who were before me in Jerusalem; also my wisdom remained with me. And whatever my eyes desired I did not keep from them; I kept my heart from no pleasure, for my heart found pleasure in all my toil, and this was my reward for all my toil."

So Solomon perfectly understood the art of what our advertising agents today call gracious living. Yet what follows immediately in the passage is a very sobering statement like a sudden splash of ice-cold water: "Then I considered all that my hands had done and the toil I had spent in doing it, and behold, all was vanity and a striving after wind, and there was nothing to be gained under the sun" (2: 4-11).

You notice that Solomon's shrill awareness of futility did not attend a life of failure but one of fabulous prosperity and success. Solomon had and did all he wanted. He satisfied his desires only to discover that what he had thought he would gain was still as remote as it had been when he started off.

After he had arrived at all his purposes he was struck with the tormenting inner conviction that that was not what he had been seeking all the time. He saw that there was a permanent gulf fixed between the realisation of his plans (which he achieved) and the ultimate aim back of his plans and actions (which he did not achieve and now knew he would never achieve).

I am certain there is no man in the world who did not from time to time make similar experiences of disillusionment. Yet when we make them we feel depressed for a while than pass on, untaught. Ecclesiastes stopped and thought. His passionate resolution to go to the root of his disillusionment makes him the great thinker and teacher he is. The book leaves no doubt that the experience of disillusionment attributed to Solomon was the author's own recurring experience. He suffered many an inner defeat, and all those defeats he sees being summed up and sealed in man's final fate.

He is indefatigable in hammering away at the fact that with all our phantastic anticipations of a fulfilment ahead our real future is one we share with the brutes: "For the fate of the sons of men and the fate of the beasts is the same; as one dies, so dies the other. They all have the same breath, and man has no advantage over the beasts; for all is vanity. All go to the same place; all are from the dust, and all turn to dust again. Who knows whether the spirit of man goes upward and the spirit of the beasts goes down to the earth?" (3: 19-21). "As he came from his mother's womb he shall go again, naked as he came, and shall take nothing for his toil, which he may carry away in his hand . . . Just as he came, so shall he go, and what gain has he that he toiled for the wind, and spent all his days in darkness and grief, in much vexation and sickness and resentment?" (5: 15-17).

Death finally unmasks the futile striving after wind at the bottom of all our cravings.

Ecclesiastes has much to say about blind acquisitiveness, insatiable greed, mutual jealousy, brutal oppression, dishonesty, corruption. Over against those vices he commends righteousness and self-control. Yet even the righteous and wise are not allowed to draw ultimate consolation from their virtues. King Solomon's disillusionment shows that even the wisest man must ultimately confess the futility of his endeavours. Also he has been striving after wind all the time. And in the end there is no difference between his fate and that of the fool: "How the wise man dies just like the fool!" (2: 16). "This also is vanity" (v. 21).

What is it that makes all our doings, wise or foolish, a striving after wind? That we reckon without our host. With all our religiousness we have not taken into account what God does and what place he has assigned to man.

Ecclesiastes' historical position is that of a bold, original thinker who could no longer seek God in the way his fathers had sought him. To the prophets of old God had revealed himself in deeds of chastisement and deliverance as he ruled over the history of his people.

At the time of Ecclesiastes Palestine was a little province under the foreign government of the capricious Ptolemeic rulers of Egypt and their corrupt underlings. It had lost what may be called, its place in history.

In order to make the faith of his fathers come alive to him Ecclesiastes had to encounter the same God in his and his fellow men's eventless every-day life.

If God is real—as he never doubted he was—one must meet him in the ordinary happenings that occur in one's experience from one day to the next. And that makes the message of this book so incisive and relevant to every man at every time.

What was the result of his quest? Did Ecclesiastes meet God? He met him as the One who resisted him. Remember today's lesson: "For everything there is a season, and a time for every matter under heaven" (3: 1). Yet as we hear later, "man does not know his time" (9: 12).

We cannot argue with him and ask him questions. We must not hanker after the meaning of our life as if that were a matter we could arrange with ourselves. We have got to do "the business that God has given to the sons of men to be busy with" (3: 10). We must start with his will, not ours, today, tomorrow and after. We must conform to the Divinely ordained juncture instead of stretching forth our hands into a vacuum. God alone rules. "He makes everything" (11: 5), filling every moment in our life-span with the content it has. Submission to him is the only remedy for our continuous escapades into a chimerical future. It is the effective check on the striving after wind that makes us miserable.

And that is what Ecclesiastes understands for the fear of God: "I know that whatever God does endures forever; nothing can be added to it, nor anything taken from it; God has made it so, in order that men should fear before him" (3: 14).

Man has neither the first word nor the last. His place is between the two, yielding and responding to the will of God which is a good will, for "God has made everything beautiful in its time" (3: 11). He does not only send us trouble. There are many enjoyments to be had, every day. The fear of him will teach us to take both, hardship and delight, from his hand. The ones we must bear as God has destined us to bear them, the others enjoy as he grants them, instead of our deferring enjoyment to a phantastic future. "In the day of prosperity be joyful and in the day of adversity consider; God has made the one as well as the other" (7: 14).

It would be wrong to complain that the balance between pleasure and pain is always in favour of the latter. For as King Solomon is represented as having observed, wisdom leads us to draw pleasure even from toiling:

"I kept my heart from no pleasure, for my heart found pleasure in all my toil, and this was my reward for all my toil" (2: 10). At this point Ecclesiastes stops. He does not hold out to us hope for a better life after death.

He does not teach immortality but rather mortality. And that is in accordance with the whole Bible. For the Bible unlike some Greek philosophers with whom Ecclesiastes probably takes issue in his book does not teach immortality as an inherent capacity of the soul.

It teaches the resurrection of the body by Divine action. But that was to be revealed later than at the time Ecclesiastes wrote. And in order to grasp what eternal life really means we must have first learned from the Old Testament to take death seriously. That is what Jesus did in weeping at the grave of Lazarus though he knew he was going to raise him. That is what Ecclesiastes can teach us with greater force and poignancy than anybody else. One might even call him a herald of the resurrection later to be revealed. For he prompts us to take our bearings from God's action and never from ourselves, all human wisdom and righteousness not-withstanding.

"Thy will be done, on earth as it is in heaven." The third clause of the Lord's prayer includes in its rich meaning the message of Ecclesiastes. For the fear of God which Ecclesiastes teaches consists in reverent surrender to his will.

Can I offer you a better New Year's message than the call to surrender to his will? I am not a glib optimist who is professionally obliged to promise you a bright, splendid future at this season of the year. I can only make this promise that is fortified not only by the teaching of the strong book under review but still more so by the gospel of the crucified and risen Saviour.

If you and I learn better to fear God, taking our directives from his will, manifest in what happens to us every day and interpreted by his word every day any stress and strain, any pain and affliction we may have to endure during this New Year will be more than compensated for by the joys God has in store to grant for us all in this year of grace and for all eternity.

LET US PRAY: Grant us, O Father, really to believe that all that comes to us comes from a Father's hand. May we better realise thy love for us, accepting its tokens in the form of both sufferings and blessings. And let us give a good account of ourselves by living the true life of thy beloved children for whom thou hast sacrificed thy Son, our Redeemer from ourselves and all evil. Amen.

iii. For Such a Time as This

(Esther 4: 14 and Acts 4: 27-30)

THE book of Esther is a very complicated product of great art. Its literary form is that of a folk story, superbly told. Its purpose is twofold, satirical and philosophical.

The object of the satire is the vast Persian empire that stretched from India to Ethiopia and under whose dominion the Jewish people lived for 200 years. The author documents an excellent first-hand knowledge of the organisation of the empire, its institutions and underlying mores. He does not criticise. He rather lets imperial despotism condemn itself. With perfect craftmanship he works his disgust at autocratic rule into his story by exaggerating many a detail till everybody must see how ridiculous the whole is even if no detail had been exaggerated.

The result is a masterly caricature that brings out the truth as in a convex mirror far more vividly than any accurate historical recording could do.

The book begins with a description of the dazzling wealth and splendour of the royal court. King Ahasuerus (Xerxes) gives a six months' banquet for the army and dignitaries that is followed by a seven-day banquet for all the male citizens that have gathered at the citadel at Susa. When the king was drunk he commanded his seven eunuch chamberlains to bring his queen, Vashti, before him with the royal crown to show the peoples and princes her beauty. As the queen was a real queen she refused to come.

The king was enraged and resolved to divorce her. He called his crown jurists who were quick to comply with his wish and supply a legal pretext for it.

The queen must be divorced by irrevocable public law lest her bad example of disobedience make all women in the kingdom to look with contempt on their husbands.

Thus every man in the kingdom was taught to be lord in his own house—by a king who himself was not lord in his own house.

After some time the king's anger abated and he wanted Vashti back as his wife. But that could not be as the laws of the Persians were all so perfect that they must never be abrogated. So his counsellors suggested that he chose a new queen out of the most beautiful maidens of his kingdom.

Throughout the kingdom girls were picked up by appointed officers and gathered to the royal harem where the eunuch in charge applied to them one whole year's beauty treatment. Having been sufficiently beautified, they were in succession brought to the king. On the following morning each one was brought to another part of the harem where she remained in seclusion unless the king should call for her again. The only exception was the one to whom the king would take such a fancy as to make her his queen.

His choice fell on a Jewish orphan by the name of Esther. Her cousin and foster-father, Mordecai, had previously charged her not to reveal her Jewish origin to any one. For by unalterable law the king could marry only a Persian. The secrecy Esther maintained about her origin, her ambitions to become queen in the ghastly way described must have appalled many a contemporary Jewish reader. We shall see that Esther is not the real hero of the book. Nor is Mordecai.

Since Mordecai was known as a Jew his kinship with Esther could not be disclosed. In order to be near her he took subordinate employment at the royal court.

One day he discovered a plot to murder the king. When he duly reported it the conspirators were executed. Mordecai was quite an unimportant person. Nobody thought of thanking him for his loyalty. The whole thing was placed on file by the court historian and that was all.

About that time the king made one Haman, an Amalekite, his grand vizier and commanded all his servants to bow down and do obeisance to him. Mordecai, however, stubbornly ignored the king's order. Haman was filled with fury and resolved to destroy not only him but his whole people throughout the kingdom. With the reason for Mordecai's stubborn refusal and Haman's deadly hate of the Jews I cannot now deal.

When by casting of lots he found an auspicious day for his noble undertaking Haman repaired to the king and asked him for a personal favour. The king should make another of his irrevocable laws with the purpose of liquidating a certain people that was dispersed in all provinces of the kingdom. Since they obeyed laws different from those of the king it was not for the king's profit to tolerate them.

In exchange for the favour received Haman proposed to do what was really for the king's profit. He offered him the fabulous sum of eighteen million dollars. The king with the noble gesture of a monarch replied that he did not care for the money, which was in polite Oriental language tantamount to acceptance of the bribe. Actually he cared so much for the money that he did not even ask Haman for the name of the people doomed to destruction. Haman had not told him and that was as well.

Haman immediately dispatched couriers to all the king's provinces with the edict "to destroy, to slay, and to annihilate all Jews, young and old, women and children" "and to plunder their goods" "in one day", eleven months from the issuing of the edict. When the couriers had left, "the king and Haman sat down to drink".

When Mordecai learned of the decreed destruction of his people he went through the prescribed routine of rending his clothes, putting on sackcloth and ashes and wailing in the midst of the city with a loud and bitter cry. Esther, being told, sent one of her eunuchs to inquire what had happened. Mordecai let her know. Esther sent him word that she could not do a thing. If she went to the king unsummoned she might forfeit her life. Mordecai challenged her to risk her life:

"If you keep silence *at such a time as this*, relief and deliverance will rise for the Jews from another quarter, but you and your father's house will perish. And who knows whether you have not come to royal estate *for such a time as this?*" Esther decided to risk her life by going to the king: "If I perish I perish". She did not express confidence in God. Nor did she ask Mordecai to pray for her.

She asked him and the Jews of Susa to keep a three-day's fast. Neither God nor prayer are mentioned in the Hebrew book of Esther. We shall see why.

When Esther came to her dread monarch he received her favourably. He held out to her the golden sceptre that was in his hand. "Then Esther approached and touched the top of the sceptre. And the king said to her: 'What is it, Queen Esther? What is your request? It shall be given you, even to the half of my kingdom'." Now that is a typical folk-tale episode. At the same time, it is a sarcastic caricature of despot's irresponsible whims.

Esther in her fear did not come out with her real request. She only asked the king to come with Haman to a dinner she had prepared. At the dinner she repeated the same request with an invitation to both for the following evening.

Her idea was thoroughly to subject the king to her charms and, at the same time, be witness of Haman's downfall.

Haman, highly flattered by the queen's repeated invitation, felt all the more infuriated when that arrogant fellow Mordecai again refused to do him obeisance. On the advice of his wife and friends he decided to erect a gallows eighty-three feet high and ask the king on the next morning to have Mordecai hanged upon it. Yet during the night in which the gallows was built curious things happened.

The king could not sleep and gave orders to bring the royal chronicles and read them before him. It happened that the servant who was reading to him hit on the story of Mordecai's loyalty in reporting a plot against the king's life. The king asked what had been the man's reward. He learned that nothing had been done for him. So he asked for one of his counsellors. *Just at this time* in the early morning Haman had arrived at the court. He came so early in order to get the king's consent to Mordecai's execution.

The king ordered him in and asked for his counsel as to how the man whom the king delighted to honour should be honoured. Haman in his vanity said to himself: "That will be I". So he suggested the most pompous and extravagant procedure. The man should be clad in royal robes, mounted on a royal horse and conducted through the open square of the city by one of the king's most noble princes, proclaiming before him: "Thus shall it be done to the man whom the king delights to honour." And this Haman had now to do to Mordecai. When he came home from the procession he covered his head, sign of impending doom.

Thus Mordecai's life is saved and the reader prepared for the following story of Haman's overthrow and the rescue of the Jewish people. I must, however, stop at this point.

What we have heard till now is enough for working out the lesson I intend to draw.

What was it that saved Mordecai's life? It was neither he himself nor Esther. On the evening of the second dinner Mordecai's corpse would have dangled from the gallows were it not for the fact that the king could not sleep the night before.

Now it happens to people in general and to folk tale kings in particular that they sometimes suffer from insomnia. But why did the king have the royal chronicles brought before him instead of a story-teller? And why did the man who was reading to him just hit on the place where Mordecai's deed was mentioned? We know why Haman came to the court so early. We also know why he misunderstood the king's question to him. This was due to his inflated and, at the same time, offended vanity. But the fact that Haman falls into his own trap and must, finally, dig his own grave is not simply due to his inflated and offended vanity. To what is it due? To whom is it due?

And here is where the anonymous hero of the Book of Esther comes in. The chief actor in this book is, at the same time, the chief actor in all books of the Bible.

And not only in the Bible. It is the purpose of the Bible to reveal him as the chief actor everywhere, in the history of the world, in your and my life-stories. And that is what makes life in a true and reverent sense, interesting. The whole real thrill of life is due to the mysterious touch of his hand. It is his touch that makes every event an event. It constitutes the reality of all experience. Take, for instance, a fascinating story to which we are listening with suspense like the one we have just heard. What makes the story tick is the touch of his hand, though most people who tell and write stories or listen to them are unconscious of it. The Bible wants to make us conscious of it. And the book of Esther is in the Bible.

Its author has a term for the Divine touch, the same term the Bible uses for it everywhere. The word is TIME: "If you keep silent at such a time as this . . . and who knows whether you have not come to royal estate for such a time as this?"

That is to say: God was at work throughout the past, leading all things up to this present challenge that compels you either to act courageously or perish miserably.

Time in its emphatic Biblical sense is the Divinely manifested juncture on which your destiny hangs, his definite call for your decision. "Such a time as this" means one at which decision is enforced upon you. How you will now decide depends on you. But decide you must. God sees to that.

There are different ways of confronting us with "such a time as this". The author of the Book of Esther is not a theologian. He is a philosophical story teller. In telling one single story he tells all stories that can be told.

The Persian court with its idiotic cultured weakling of a king bares and reveals the structure of this pompous, stupid and dangerously cruel world. This world will forever presume to run a course of its own. Nonsense. It is the Divine touch that runs it, and any true picture of this world brings the Divine touch home to us. The true philosopher need not mention the name of God. God is there, whenever the world is taken for what it is and pictured accordingly. The writer of Esther preaches God indirectly and he is consistent enough to stick to his indirect method of making room for God as he reveals himself through the things he has done and is doing all the time.

It is not the lesson of the Book of Esther that we should systematically and meticulously scan our experiences for traces of special Divine providence. There are such traces as we all know. Their purpose is not to satisfy our curiosity or provide an emotional uplift. That miraculous escape you still vividly remember after so many years—what does it really mean? A Divine challenge to live your whole life in the light of what you perfectly understood *at that time*. The time of felt Divine intervention sets the pattern for our whole life-time.

The conspicious events are meant to focus out attention not on themselves but rather on the ordinary ones. Through all that is and happens the Lord God seeks to awaken us to meet him. It is he with whom we have always to do.

He is our light and law, our help and salvation, the meaning of all. If the Book of Esther has helped us to see him approach us everywhere we have understood its main message.

LET US PRAY: We thank thee, our Lord, who hast been wooing for our hearts ever since we were made. We confess to thee our blindness and inertia and the insincerity of our hearts in trying to by-pass thee. We acknowledge our punishments in that the life we have led is so unreal.

Quicken us with thy presence and may we attain to living the true life that can only be lived in thy presence through Jesus Christ our Redeemer. Amen.

iv. Thanksgiving on a Day of Mourning

(Psalm 103: 2 and Rev. 22: 1-5)

THE man who composed the One hundred and third Psalm was of like nature with ourselves. Sometimes he felt grateful to God, at other times he was so overwhelmed with grief and sorrow that he could not get himself to praising God as he knew he ought to. At the time of this Psalm he must have been in a depressed mood of mind. Though we don't know the date, neither the year nor even the century, the Psalmist's hope that the Lord "will not always chide, nor will he keep his anger for ever" points to a trying national crisis. The situation must have looked desperate.

The Psalmist had, however, been taught to praise the Lord always, in season and out of season. He knew and understood it that the worship of God with thanksgiving and praise at its centre must never be deferred to a seemingly more congenial occasion.

The praise of God is not a matter of fleeting emotion. There is always occasion for it. It is not true, said the Psalmist to himself, that there is not reason for me to praise God now. "Bless the Lord, O my soul," he says, arousing himself from the natural man's spiritual stupor, "and all that is within me, bless his holy name."

Thus he wakened himself though not quite. He continued his soliloquy, pleading earnestly with himself, rebuking his sluggish, obtuse soul of the most hideous of all sins, ingratitude: "Bless the Lord, O my soul, and forget not all his benefits".

Doesn't that speak to our present condition? Who among us finds himself in a proper mood for celebrating Thanksgiving two days after the President's assassination? How can we feel grateful after what happened on Friday last week? How could it have happened? Don't we call on God as the Protector of our nation? Couldn't he have prevented that ghastly, foul deed?

My answer to these desperate questions is that we should know better. Actually we did know better, all of us, at the very moment when the terrible news was broken to us. A moment earlier we may have harboured all kinds of everyday trivial thoughts: selfish cares mixed with daydreams, wishful thinking, foolish desires and resentments, fears, and then, at once when we learned of the President's death something radically different struck us.

What was it? A consciousness of reality, not the mock reality that presumes upon us for most of the time, but true reality. For most of the time we are living in an imaginary world of flimsy excuses and self-defences. Suddenly, for a crucial moment all this is exploded, as we are being exposed to a powerful Divine message that shatters the walls of false security and conceit, reducing us to the position of helpless little children, shivering and crying in an ice-cold, fallen world.

'How could this have happened?' 'Only a mad man could have done it.' 'A sinister conspiracy.' 'Woe to America.' 'Woe to the whole world.' All these are only second thoughts with which we already try to escape from the severe shock we experienced and which is no more and no less than the shock of reality itself. We try to make ourselves forget that we live in a world and are with our whole being attached to a world of lie and murder, a world that once and for all revealed its nature by crucifying the Son of God. The sudden impact of the horrible news bears the meaning and has the force of a divine call to seriousness: in realising our humble position before God, in repenting of our irresponsibility, in delivering up ourselves into the hand of God with whom we have to do.

Isn't this severe reminder a great divine benefit? How can we refuse to see a benefit in what is destined to lead us from falsehood to truth, from fickleness to resolute faith, from taking it easy to meeting our God? Unless we were in dire need of being taught this lesson the Lord would not have administered it to us. Yet we can truly benefit by it only if we don't forget but remember it as the Psalmist instructs us: "Forget not all his benefits".

"Praise the Lord, O my soul, and forget not all his benefits."

In order to better understand the message that the present divine visitation conveys we must further heed the Psalmist's instruction: "All his benefits," he says, then enumerates some of them. Yet there is one among them with which he starts and on which he dwells in the main part of the Psalm. What is it?

Neither health, nor prosperity nor vigorous life, Divine gifts for which he gives due praise to the Giver. But the central gift from which all the others receive their definite meaning and to which I wish to draw your devout attention at this celebration of Thanksgiving is not of an external nature. What is it? Let us listen to the Psalmist: "Bless the Lord, O my soul, and all that is within me, bless his holy name. Bless the Lord, O my soul, and forget not all his benefits, who forgives all your iniquity".

M*

The main reason for praising God on every occasion, be it glad or be it as sad as our present plight, is his revealed mercy in forgiving our sins.

May we all in availing ourselves of this sacred testimony follow the Psalmist in putting first things first. In order to look into the future with sober confidence as behoves us at Thanksgiving we must humble ourselves before our Maker and Ruler, asking him to forgive our sins as a nation. For what is at the root of our present calamity? What made the stern message we have received necessary? The Psalmist testifies: "He made known his ways to Moses, his acts to the people of Israel".

Do we as a nation care for the ways of God made known to us? We may a thousand times call ourselves a religious people, but that will not exempt us from judgment unless our religion produces the fruit of moral integrity, honesty, real concern for the common good, brotherliness, compassion for all who suffer. Remember what is elegantly called 'conflicts of interest' in Congress and on all levels of government. Remember our migrant workers. Remember the seventy million Americans, forty per cent. of our total population, who have no share in our present prosperity but subsist on a marginal income. And what about racial discrimination? Is there anything more urgent on this day than to ask God to forgive us and grant us some strong stimuli for making amends?

And who should pray for forgiveness except the church? The nation as such does not do it or does not do its consistently. For the nation as a nation does not add its Amen of conviction to the Psalmist's confession:

"For he knows our frame; he remembers that we are dust." "We are dust," confesses the Psalmist on behalf of his people. 'What?' 'Dust?' 'We are Americans.' The Bible teaches us, here and elsewhere, that we are dust. "Behold, the nations are like a drop from a bucket and are accounted as the dust on the scales," we read in the prophet who showed a profound concern for the salvation of the nations, the second Isaiah (40: 15).

"We are dust." Is that what you hear at any one of our political gatherings? Or at a meeting of the Parents Teachers Association? The church is the place where it can and must be confessed. The church is the place where not only the futility but the positive sinfulness of the nation must be brought before God with the humble cry for forgiveness and restoration.

The church must vicariously repent on behalf of the nation. Only if we do can we draw from the word of God the confidence in his forbearing, upholding grace that inspires the present Psalm: "The Lord is merciful and gracious, slow to anger and abounding in steadfast love. He will not always chide, nor will he keep his anger for ever. He does not deal with us according to our sins, nor requite us according to our iniquities. For as the heavens are high above the earth, so great is his steadfast love toward those who fear him; as far as the east is from the west, so far does he remove our transgressions from us. As a father pities his children, so the Lord pities those who fear him."

Our Lord and Saviour said: "Whoever exalts himself will be humbled and whoever humbles himself will be exalted" (Mt. 23: 12).

As the Psalmist had humbled himself with his confession and intercession on behalf of his people he was exalted. He was revealed the most comforting, in a sense the only comforting, truth about the history of his nation and of every nation, one that is always valid and which he stated with absolute certitude: "The Lord has established his throne in the heavens, and his kingdom rules over all".

Who rules over the world? Who is going to decide upon its destiny during this critical period of history? America? Russia? The United Nations? There is only One who rules. Who is he, and what is his character? The Lord, "merciful and gracious, slow to anger and abounding in steadfast love".

To this great Lord let us in humble penitence entrust the future of our nation. To him let us offer our gratitude and praise for all his dealings with us, most of all for the fatherly goodness and forgiving patience with which he has borne and instructed us up to this day. If we do we will celebrate Thanksgiving in a serious but no less joyful mood of mind. For seriousness and joy are not at all opposed to one another. They are inseparably united through the bond that holds together the Cross and the resurrection of our all-loving, all-powerful, eternally victorious Saviour.

LET US PRAY: We confess to thee, our Maker, Ruler and Saviour our sins of fickleness, irresponsibility, confusion of seriousness and play, vain presumption, racial pride and discrimination, vanity, favouritism, dishonesty, crime. And we beseech thee, to forgive us and grant us the regenerative power to be true to what is good in our history and worth imitation. Comfort those who mourn, especially the late President's family and all who were near to him. And grant the new President wisdom and authority to direct our affairs for the good of our nation and of the whole world. For the sake of Christ in whom we trust. Amen.

v. Until I Had Brought Him Into My Mother's House

(Song of Songs 3: 1-5)

THIS passage describes a dream—the dream of a young married woman who transports herself back to the time of her betrothal. She lives it all over again. Again she suffers the tortures of a love not yet sure of the right response. Once again her heart throbs in the restlessness of misunderstanding and being misunderstood, in the fear of possible loss—in anxious seeking and searching. Now that the waiting time is over this nightmare serves only to increase the enjoyment of her present happiness. As she awakes she knows that she is doubly happy. For the dark background of the past throws in relief the brightness of the present. "If I should be without him then I should have to jump from my couch in the middle of the night and run through the dark streets; stand before coarse watchmen and let myself be thought of as a mad woman. And when I found him, I would hold him and never let him go, until I brought him into my mother's house!"

When we feel somehow or other supremely happy we seem to be in a dream. It was otherwise with the singer of this song. Her feelings were sounder. To her the terrible time of the past is an empty dream and the happiness of the present a waking reality. Yet she feels the past as if it were present—in a dream. How remarkable that this, a happy woman, should still dream and should need to dream. In her dream the light of the happiness of her love calls up the shadow of love's yearnings, for this is necessary in order to make the light supremely bright. Even the delight of the happiest love does need something to increase it. The present cannot dispense with the past, with the backward glance, with the contrasts—if it would be in harmony. And thus we come to the frontier, the brittleness of earthly happiness. The soul of man is like a leaking vessel. The precious liquid which is poured into it causes a fragrance to issue from it; but it is just enough to sip. The dream buttresses the unstable present by means of the past. But in order that a man should stand upright and progress, he must have a glimpse of a future which is free from the limitations and infirmities of the present time. This life points beyond itself and even the best it gives us is but an earnest of the future and is essentially to be valued thus. Time without eternity is empty. Time lived in the light of eternity is but a preparation for it.

So this wonderful love song, taken even at its own valuation, points beyond itself to that love of which earthly love is but an image, the better the image the purer and stronger it is. "For love is strong as death; jealousy is cruel as the grave; the coals thereof are coals of fire which has a most vehement flame. Many waters cannot quench love, neither can the floods drown it; if a man would give all the substance of his house for love it would utterly be condemned" (Cant. 8: 6-7).

Paul was thinking of this when he wrote the thirteenth chapter of the First Letter to the Corinthians, and so we may understand, why the Song of Songs, a collection of Old Israelite wedding hymns was received into the Canon of Holy Scriptures. Earthly love is the nearest and the most natural image of God's love.

Therefore we are justified and constrained to look beyond the literal interpretation of the text to the spiritual interpretation which it claims as part of the Holy Scriptures.

If we then were to dream that we had not yet found him whom our soul loveth, even Christ, that we would once again have to go and seek him, then we would put ourselves back in spirit into that terrible time of conflict.

We have found the Messiah because he has sought us, but he finds only those who allow themselves to be found by him, that is those who have sought him. Most certainly we should never have found him, had he not sought us: we should never have reached up to him, had he not gone forth to seek us.

Nevertheless, he to whom all power is given in heaven and on earth withheld himself, had to withhold himself, from finding souls which refused to seek him. He is ever ready to let himself be found by all who seek him, because his seeking moved their hearts. We know this because it has been revealed to us; but from knowledge, even knowledge supported by faith, to certainty of experience founded on faith there is a long road of spiritual struggles—a wandering that leads through many a dark night, along the edge of more than one precipice, a sailing between the Scylla of pride, which does not want to let itself be found, and the Charybdis of laziness which finds seeking too much trouble. Till we reach our goal we have to suffer anguish of heart, a condition of which many a passage in the Song of Songs bears witness. We must also expect to be counted as fools by the world—the world within us and the world without us —like the girl who gets at night out of her bed and wanders through the dark lanes and squares, detained and laughed to scorn by the night-watchmen, the strict, the narrow-minded, the straw-splitters, the tattlers and the talebearers. Yet the testimony to the night-watchmen, "Have you not seen him whom my soul loveth?", however foolish it may seem to them, need not have been in vain. It is a path which nobody who has once trod it would care to tread again. But now the goal is reached. "The darkness is past and the true light now shineth" (1 Jn. 2: 8). Now we know and testify joyfully in the words of the Song of Songs: "My friend is mine and I am his". So the 'dream' with its recollections of the dark years of our conversion time serves to fill our hearts with glad gratitude and doubles our appreciation of our present salvation in Jesus Christ.

And yet we are like the dreaming woman of the Song. The fact is, we need the backward glance at our past struggles, in order to appreciate our present spiritual possessions. We require the contrast to what lies behind to help us to a deeper joy in our present salvation. This fact brings out clearly the insufficiency and the fragility—not of the salvation freely bestowed on us in Christ, but of our present appropriation of this salvation. The Christianity of us all, measured with the rod of Scriptures, leaves much to be desired. This and the daily Cross of life in a world which scorns the redemption, and the daily Cross of suffering with this world and for her keeps us tense as we look with the eye of faith into the future. "We are saved by hope," says Paul (Rom. 8: 24); "but hope that is seen is not hope, for what a man seeth why doth he yet hope for? But if we hope for that we see not, then do we with patience wait for it." The insufficiency and fragility of the present should teach us the right waiting. "Let your loins be girded about, and your lights burning; and ye yourselves like unto men who wait for their Lord" (Lk. 12: 35 f.).   Let us wait soberly for the wedding feast which our King prepares for his bride—the Church.   Let us as those who have been reconciled with God wait earnestly for the full redemption of the coming Kingdom.

This wedding feast can only be celebrated after we have "brought into the house of our mother" him whom our soul loveth.   The bringing in of the beloved "into the chamber of her that conceived me" is not yet the wedding but precedes it.   In our song the loving one thinks first of her mother, when love has grown to maturity in her heart.   The mother is the deepest confidant of the daughter. She shall know of her love and take her into her protection.

Also this we should understand spiritually in referring to the Church of Christ.   The mother of the Church is Israel: at the time of her first love the Church has left nothing undone to lead her heavenly Bridegroom to her mother.   She found no response; her mother behaved as if she were a wicked step-mother.   And when the time of the first love had passed, without a new access of spiritual love, the daughter just returned to her mother like-for-like: she behaved like a step-daughter.   The mother may deny the daughter and the daughter the mother; yet the mother will find no rest until she has received her daughter's heavenly Bridegroom into her house, and likewise the daughter will find no rest until she has brought him, whom her soul loveth into her mother's house.   As long as this has not happened, she cannot have a quiet conscience.   This is not in relation to her love and vow, because they are fixed for ever in heaven; but rather in relation to her mother.   Has the daughter really done everything she could, with patient and true persistence, to bring the blessing of her mother upon this marriage contract?   If she had done so, then everything would be better for her.

But now she must not take her ease and rest until the day comes when both mother and daughter are one in their joy over this wedding.   To recognise this, and with tireless faithfulness to bring it about, "in season and out of season" (2 Tim. 4: 2).   "In much patience . . . in afflictions, in necessities, in distress . . . by pureness, by knowledge, by longsuffering, by kindness, by the Holy Ghost, by love unfeigned, by the word of truth, by the power of God, by the armour of righteousness on the right hand and on the left, by honour and dishonour, by evil report and good report: as deceivers and yet true, as unknown and yet well known" (2 Cor. 6: 4, 6-9).

This is the duty of the Church so far as her mission to Israel is concerned.

This task of the Church has for us Christians out of Israel a particular significance. As members of the Church we have the same duty as all other members: of obedience to the missionary order of the Church toward Israel. But as—at the same time —we know and recognise that Israel is our mother according to the flesh, we have a personal motive in the missionary endeavour of the Church toward Israel.

We Christians out of Israel are children who have been cast out by our earthly mother. Should we therefore forget her? Should we return like for like? Can we cease to be grateful to our mother? We owe her gratitude though she is erring, though she may curse her own flesh and blood. If we had nothing else to be grateful for (and there are other causes for gratitude), we must be grateful to her, that she is our mother according to God's providence and ordering. That is why it must pain us far more deeply than believers from among the Gentiles that our mother has not recognised the covenant of love which the Crucified has made with us all. "If I forget thee, O Jerusalem, let my right hand forget her cunning" (Ps. 137: 5). Whoever throws over his mother throws over himself. That holds good for the Church in regard to Israel, and it has for us Christians out of Israel an even more obvious and corporal meaning.

For the sake of this contract, this new covenant, we Christians out of Israel are called as members of the Church to work on the evangelisation of Israel just as are all others. We are not called because we are particularly gifted, or that our service ensures greater results, but the general Christian call comes home to us, personally, on account of our ancestry. This general Christian task calls us in a tone of particular warmth, for which we should be grateful. This ought to make us happier and more faithful in the carrying out of our service, as we stand in that place where God has called us. It gives us no greater joy than where its privilege is of doing what God has commanded.

In closing I would like to refer briefly to the last verse of the passage, "I charge you . . ." (Song of Songs 3: 5). It does not belong anymore to the dream of the young woman, but rather to the description of the wedding. For us who live in the Orient, the literal interpretation of the verse causes no difficulties. The happy pair ask but for a little peace from the deafening noises of an oriental wedding feast.

We can apply this also in a quite simple way to our service. Let us be on guard against that noise and bustle which only distracts in spite of our best intentions. True love is quiet and strong without needing any stimulus. She works in the stillness and even where she carries out her service with full publicity she brings her own peculiar stillness over all. "Love is not puffed up" (1 Cor. 13: 4). Restlessness and noise are always to be found where men are working up something instead of waiting in faith for the Divine creative act. When we in the sober execution of our duty as witnesses preserve the Divine quietness, our heart in all weakness and temptation will again and again be filled with Divine comfort. We shall hasten on to that day, when Israel will gladly open the doors of house and chamber to him, whom our soul loveth and who first loved us; who embraces Israel from the beginning to the end of her history in a passionate, patient, unceasing and ever victorious love.

vi. How to Live in the Present World

(1 Corinthians 7: 29-31 and John 17: 6, 9-17)

THE appointed time is the time of grace granted us before the course of this world will come to an end. Throughout Church history up to the present day attempts have been made to compute the end. How long will the time of grace last? When are the last days going to begin? All these attempts have failed and they should never have been made. For the answer to the questions raised is already provided by the New Testament. As to the duration of the last time the present text reveals that it is very short. As to the period between now and the beginning of the last days—there is no such period.

For according to the New Testament we are already now living in the last time.

Then, however, one might ask how the last time could be called very short. For since the apostle wrote this epistle 1900 years have already passed, and nobody knows how many more years will pass before the end comes.

The answer to this question is that time with Paul and other New Testament writers does not have the physical, impersonal meaning in which the term is mostly used. Time is not clock time but moral time, the time of opportunity, the time of crucial decision. That the time of grace has run very short, means then that there is no more time left for further stalling, detours, excuses.

Either you walk on the narrow path Christ has opened for you, or else you will have missed your opportunity for ever. Choose between life and death now before it is too late! "The appointed time has grown very short." The text stands at the beginning of the brief portion that was part of today's New Testament lesson. What follows in this portion cannot be grasped apart from the text. Paul admonishes the married men to live as those who have no wives. Those who mourn should do it as those who do not mourn, those who rejoice as people who do not rejoice. The buyers of goods should feel and act like the ones who have no goods.

Now these were only a few examples selected by the apostle with the purpose of illustrating his point. They are followed by a summary that lays down the rule for the whole Christian life. Paul writes that all our dealings with the world should be conducted in a manner that comes up to having no dealings at all with it.

This can be easily misunderstood. Paul does not say that married people should love one another not too much, or that grief and joy should be watered down, or that our economic affairs should not be taken seriously but rather dealt with in a negligent manner. He is not a teacher of anaemic, boring detachment. The gospel he proclaims has far more to offer than a spirit of weak resignation and passiveness.

He concludes the passage with a statement that can greatly help us to understand the preceding admonitions.

"This world in its present form is passing away." Notice the close connection with the present text: "The appointed time has grown very short".

Now if this world in its present form is rapidly passing away— what then will remain? The answer is according to Paul and the whole New Testament: Love only.

Because love is the only thing that lasts, this whole unloving world will soon be no more. The consequence to be drawn from this central fact consists in conquering the outlook, the attitudes and actions that are characteristic of this unloving world.

For instance: To live in Christian matrimony is to enjoy the blessings of mutual love in closest personal vicinity. To the worldly mind, however, that besets us all, one's wife or husband means the nearest object on which to impose one's own will. Therefore, you Christians, lead your matrimonial life as those who are not married in the sense of the world.

Further: To mourn to express grief: To the worldly mind in us all it means unbounded despair soon changing into irresponsible light-mindedness. Don't mourn like the world!

Again: Joy is the greatest divine gift to the soul: Worldly joy is so vulgar and shallow that the sounds it makes over our radio stations twenty-four hours a day represents no more than yawns of tedious, trivial languish. Don't join in the world's phony joy!

Our economic activities serve the purpose of meeting our own life necessities and those of others: The world is a grasper, never satisfied, always craving for more and more. Don't engage in this mad hunt! Greedy and vain competition makes this world an affray of ruthless claims and counter claims that cancel out one another.

"This world in its present form is passing away," as it is grinding itself to death. It has never been and will never be truly alive.

The Christians are called and privileged to live real lives in a dead world. The true husband knows that he owns his wife no more than she owns him. The Christian mourner expresses with his mourning the inestimable worth of what he has lost yet knows at the same time that more than he can ever lose will finally be restored to him by his merciful Father in heaven.

Pure joy in all its forms is the loving delight taken in the treasures of Creation and Redemption. Love also put its stamp on the hard struggle for economic survival. It purifies the spirit of competition with the consideration of one's competitors' rights and with the care for the common good.

Jesus said in his high priestly prayer that his disciples are in the world but not of the world. The material of worldly unlovingness with which they have constantly to deal is transformed by them through the worshipful love for God and the loving, active identification with their fellow men.

Does Paul recommend a pale, reduced existence of melancholic withdrawal?

No, he reveals the mystery of real living with its real trouble and pain and with its real happiness and joy to which there is no end.   The appointed time that has grown very short is the time for starting the only true life.   What the apostle commends is not tired acquiescence but radiant fulfilment.

The start of the new life cannot be deferred to the world to come. For how can one continue in eternity with what he has not started now during this very short time of crucial decision?   "The appointed time has grown very short."   It need not be extended, for already now the gift of radical renewal is offered us and the power to decide for its acceptance is granted us by Jesus Christ our Redeemer from sin and death.   May we all receive the supreme blessing of his sacrament with the earnest desire to be renewed into the image of the loving God.   Amen.

LET US PRAY: O Almighty God, who pourest on all who desire it the spirit of grace and supplication; deliver us, when we draw nigh to thee, from coldness of heart and wanderings of mind; that with steadfast thoughts and kindled affections, we may worship thee in spirit and truth.   Amen.

10. What Makes a Normal Christian?

(Romans 12: 11 and Deut. 6: 1-13; Rev. 3: 14-22)

WHAT DO PEOPLE in general understand for a normal Christian? One who keeps to the accepted standards of Christian faith and conduct. He believes in the Bible, goes to Church, contributes to the Church. He is a moral person, he is also a kind person. In all that he avoids extravagance. He fights shy of what smacks of fanaticism, exaltation or an overly emotional atmosphere. He always steers a sound middle-course of moderation. He is therefore considered a respectable and reliable man—though I wonder if there is anything about his Christianity that could be called exciting.

What does the apostle Paul understand for a normal Christian? "Never flag in zeal," he writes.

To Paul, a typical Christian is a man filled with zeal for God. The apostle is writing to a congregation he had never met personally. But that they have zeal for God he takes simply for granted. He does not tell them that they ought to have zeal. He only exhorts them never to let the zeal which they already have slacken. Zeal is to him the normal thing.

What shall we say to that? I believe we shall have to say that the apostle's standards of normal Christianity were very different from ours. A Christianity of which zeal is one of the typical characteristics is a very exciting phenomenon. Compared with the fervour and enthusiasm of the early Christians our ideas of what is normal bear the stamp of tedious mediocrity.

This impression is strengthened by what follows in our text: "Be aglow with the Spirit". Are we aglow with the Spirit? Is not our spiritual climate rather one of general tepidity with some scattered emotional flares? To glow means, however, to burn all the time with a strong and continued heat. As to the nature and origin of this order the apostle does not leave us in doubt: "Be aglow with the Spirit". Spirit with capital S. The Spirit of God covets to

193

make us into spiritual beings, wholly dedicated to God, glowing for him with unquenched zeal.

And that leads us to the third part of our text on which the lines drawn so far converge: "Serve the Lord". We must never flag in zeal, we must be aglow with the Spirit in order to serve the Lord.

What it means to serve the Lord and what should constrain us to serve the Lord is set forth in clear and passionate language at the beginning of this chapter: "I appeal to you, therefore, brethren by the mercies of God to present yourselves as a living sacrifice, holy and acceptable to God, which is your spiritual worship". The apostle's appeal to serve the Lord in spiritual worship draws its whole force from the mercies of God. Because God has shown us mercy we must serve him as living sacrifices. Now when Paul speaks of the mercy of God he does not think in general terms. He thinks precisely of the saving deed of God in Christ, his sacrifice on the Cross. Because God has given himself to us in Christ our whole life must be a response to his deed of mercy. As God has given his all to us we must give our all to him. And this holy and acceptable sacrifice we must make without reserve, everywhere, all the time. "When you sit in your house, and when you walk by the way and when you lie down and when you rise" (Dt. 6: 7).

Our total surrender to God in response to his loving mercy cannot be made with clenched teeth. There can be nothing cramped, affected or artificial about our spiritual worship. Nor should we think of it in terms of conspicuous heroic efforts. God rather claims the whole of our ordinary day by day life. Take for instance *eating*. How can we serve the Lord in eating our food? The austere ascetic would say, 'Eat of the most frugal meal and as little as possible and without taking delight in it'. But that makes God into a grudger and habitual no-sayer. The moralist would say: 'Eat moderately'. That's right, but mere moderation does not make eating a sacrifice to God. Say grace at table and mean it. After having said grace do not go back on your gratitude. Bring the two together and keep them together, your enjoyment of the food God has given to you and your joyful gratitude to the Giver who has shown you his saving love in Jesus Christ. Let your prayer of thanksgiving shape the satisfaction of your natural appetite, and you will have offered yourself to God as a living sacrifice.

Here is another instance of spiritual worship: How can we serve God in suffering? If we suffer pain in our body or in our mind we must offer ourselves to our Father in taking it from his hand. Remember Job when the messengers brought him the horrible news of the sudden death of all his children: "Shall we receive good at the hand of God, and shall we not receive evil?" (2: 10). We cannot sugar our pains. Let us hold fast to the truth that our affliction comes from the hand of a loving, almighty Father of inscrutable wisdom whose whole mind is revealed to us in the death of his Son. Let us insist that he has in no respect ceased to care for us and be concerned for us now. If we bring our faith and our pain together and keep them together we surrender ourselves to God as a living sacrifice.

I have cited only two instances of serving the Lord, and I leave it to you to draw the conclusions that extend to different areas of life. We must serve God by offering ourselves to him in our daily drudgery and boring routine. We must also offer him our feelings of satisfaction in the healthy performance of simple duties. All the work of our hands ought to be spiritual worship rendered to the Father of the Lord Jesus Christ. Only so can we render effective, loving service to our neighbour. It is true that we chiefly serve God by serving our neighbour. But it is no less true that in order to live for our neighbour we must be spiritual entities and not mere zeroes. By giving ourselves to God we are made available to him as instruments for extending his active love to whomever we meet.

And all this through Jesus Christ, the Giver of the new heart, who with his Gospel and Spirit kindles in us a holy passion for returning ourselves to our Father. As God lives for us we must live for Him.

God has given us his Son and with him the power to live for him. And to live for God is the secret of real, everlasting happiness.

LET US PRAY: O God, our only help and hope, we confess to thee that our life is far below what is normal in thy sight. Grant us, we beseech thee, to receive thy gift of grace and to appropriate it by practising what thou givest. Teach us to prepare in our prayers for everything we have to do or suffer and may the spirit of prayer fill our attitude and actions. Let us progress day by day in training for eternal life in the blessed fellowship with thee and him whom thou hast sent, Jesus Christ our Lord and Redeemer. Amen.